REINVENTING RESILIENCE

REINVENTING RESILIENCE

HOW ORGANIZATIONS MOVE BEYOND SETBACKS AND GROW THROUGH CHALLENGES

Paul Thallner

NEW DEGREE PRESS
COPYRIGHT © 2022 PAUL THALLNER
All rights reserved.

REINVENTING RESILIENCE
*How Organizations Move beyond Setbacks
and Grow through Challenges*

ISBN
979-8-88504-591-9 *Paperback*
979-8-88504-936-8 *Kindle Ebook*
979-8-88504-825-5 *Digital Ebook*

*With gratitude to
Varick Van Wyck Stringham III
for his courage and confidence*

Contents

INTRODUCTION	**13**
Staring into the Valley	13
An Inspired Take on Resilience	15
The Model	16
My First Glimpse at a Workplace	17
Stress at Work	18
My Research	20
What's in It for you?	21
Why Me?	22
Chapter Road Map	24
CHAPTER 1: DEFINING RESILIENCE	**29**
Overwhelm	29
Saving the Ski Industry	30
Evolution of the Model	33
Neuroscience of Resilience	35
Today's Workplace Threat Response	38
The Insidious Amygdala Hijack	40
Resilience Insights	41

Conclusion	42
Chapter Summary	43
CHAPTER 2: WE'RE DOING THIS WRONG	**45**
Questions Are Fateful	45
Problem-Solving in Organizations	47
Gap Closing Cycles	48
In Lieu of Fixing	49
Breaking Free from Gap-Closing Cycles	52
Killing Pygmalion	54
We Can Do It Right	56
Chapter Summary	57
CHAPTER 3: THE WORKPLACE STRESS EPIDEMIC	**59**
The Gales	59
Stronger Storms	64
More Change	**65**
The Price of Adaptability	66
Mindfulness and Workplace Stress	67
When the Wind Howls, Be Dutch	68
Chapter Summary	69
CHAPTER 4: HOW RESILIENCE SCALES	**71**
It's All About We	71
Resilience Scales	72
The Case: Jay Peak Mountain Resort	75
Resilience at Scale Insights	81
Chapter Summary	82

CHAPTER 5: THE LIFE-GIVING SOURCE OF RESILIENCE — 85

But My People Are Resilient — 85
The Perniciousness of Narratives — 87
The Estuary of Resilience — 88
What Collective Efficacy Looks Like — 89
How to Lose Collective Efficacy — 92
What Staunch Realism Looks Like — 94
How to Lose Staunch Realism — 98
Brackish Water of Resilience — 99
Chapter Summary — 100

CHAPTER 6: COURAGE — 103

What is Courage? — **104**
How to Build Organizational Courage — 105
Identify and Address Blockers — 105
Understand and Accept the Situation — 108
Courage in Action:
Protagonist Therapeutics' Moment of Truth — 112
A Courage Parable: Carrots, Eggs, and Coffee — 117
Courage at Scale — 118
Chapter Summary — 119

CHAPTER 7: CONFIDENCE — 121

Fake it Until You Make it? — 121
What Is Confidence? — 122
How to Build Organizational Confidence — 123
Access Resources — 124
Discover Possibilities — 127
Confidence in Action: All American Entertainment — 130

Confidence in Command: The USS Benfold 133
Confidence in History: Shackleton
and the Crew of the Endurance 135
Confidence Can Scale 139
Chapter Summary 139

CHAPTER 8: LIFE IN THE ESTUARY **141**
Rejecting Resilience's Paradox 142
Organizations Are Human Systems 143
A Resilience Tour 144
Of Life Cycles and Estuaries 152
Chapter Summary 153

CHAPTER 9: DWELLING IN POSSIBILITY **155**
Change Brings Possibility 155
The Story of My Name 156
Valley to Valley 157
Bliss in the Abyss 159
Resilience in Conflict: California's Standards War 161
Resilience and Time: Slovakia's Transformation 163
Throwing Open the Windows of Possibility 165
Chapter Summary 166

CONCLUSION **167**
Collective Efficacy + Staunch Realism 168
Courage and Confidence 169
It's Time to Reinvent Resilience 170
What to Do Now 171

ACKNOWLEDGMENTS **175**

APPENDIX **179**

Introduction

STARING INTO THE VALLEY

I was sure I was going to die. I could not take another step. We arrived at a particularly difficult section three days into my hike through the Grand Canyon. It was like we were hiking laterally across a vertical wall. To the right of the twelve-inch-wide footpath was the soaring face of the canyon wall so steep my shoulders brushed against it as I walked. To the left, a sharp drop-off of about six hundred feet into a yawning chasm below.

Something happened. I stopped. I couldn't move my feet. I started hyperventilating. I could feel the sweat on my brow for the first time in the arid daytime sun. I looked up, attempting to gather my thoughts, and all I saw was an eagle gliding effortlessly in the sky. It brought a sudden memory of my late brother-in-law Rick who died in a paragliding accident. I began to unravel at the unfairness of his death, and my nerves began fraying fast. "Oh shit," I thought. "I'm going to die. I'm going to fall right into that chasm, never to be seen again."

Our guide, Adam, noticed I was in trouble and walked back to where I had stopped. He asked if I was okay.

"Nope, I'm having a panic attack," I told him. I was terrified and didn't think I could move.

He said, "Okay. No problem. This happens a lot at this part of the trail. It's pretty intimidating. But everyone gets through it just fine, and you will too. I'll help you."

Adam got to work helping me regain control of my triggered brain. He asked me questions and got me to talk about people I love, skills I have, or groups I like hanging out with. We kept talking as I shuffled through the tricky part of the trail. It was masterful how he kept me out of react mode by bringing my thinking brain back online. He helped me see the possibility of getting through that section, and he did it by being honest about the reality of the situation.

Adam didn't give me anything I didn't possess already, but he helped me find my footing. He helped me summon the courage to face the harsh reality of the situation—it was seriously dangerous—as well as the triggers that paralyzed me. He also enabled my confidence to access the resources I had at hand: him, of course, but also my hiking ability, the fact I'd already survived several days below the rim, and the solid ground beneath my feet.

The experience on the trail changed something in me. Proceeding from that point felt like bonus time—like I left an old version of myself behind and walked forward with a new belief and purpose. I had changed.

I began to think about resilience in the context of my experience in the canyon. *Bouncing back* seemed to mischaracterize the experience. I didn't simply survive that moment. I grew because of it.

AN INSPIRED TAKE ON RESILIENCE

As an organizational change expert, I tend to look for meaning in context. Naturally, I started thinking about my experience in the canyon through that lens. What could that experience teach me about how organizations face difficult challenges?

With the volume and intensity of change increasing and the inevitability of organizations facing their own Grand Canyon moments, I started wondering what makes an organization resilient.

That hike planted the seeds of this book, as well as twenty-five years of working with organizations to help them become places where people thrive. I discovered two things as I reflected on my experience and researched this book. First, the way we use the word *resilience* does not adequately capture the growth and change that happens when we experience a difficult moment. We limit our use of the word to simply *bouncing back*.

Second, from an organizational perspective, the literature focuses largely on workers' responsibility to develop resilience. Doing so, popular opinion says, will help organizations become more resilient. However, relying on workers to build their resilience avoids the real issue. If organizations' cultures were better, workers would not need to bounce back from setbacks so often or with such effort.

I believe we need to reinvent resilience. If we create resilient organizations, maybe we could lighten the load on workers, reduce stress, and increase well-being. So, I developed the model below that provides a useful framework for understanding resilience at the organizational level. I used thinking and research from people who studied resilience and sought to apply it at scale.

I redefine resilience as *the courage and confidence to grow through challenges*. My model illustrates how resilience is:

Scalable. Resilience strategies apply to teams, organizations, communities, and even countries.

Strengths-based. We've been thinking about resilience backward. We've focused on our deficits rather than our resources that allow us to do much more than bounce back.

Storable. Discovering our resilience when we're flat on our face leaves too much to chance. Resilience is a set of qualities that can be strengthened and stockpiled.

Sustainable. Resilience is not simply about surviving challenges but recognizing our courage and confidence to grow through them and be better prepared for future headwinds.

Strategic. Above all, intentionally building organizational resilience—instead of hoping it's there when needed—can be road mapped and incorporated into organizational systems.

THE MODEL

An organization builds resilience when it has a strong core that consists of keen awareness of its internal and external environments and the forces acting on them (**staunch**

realism), as well as a strong shared belief the organization will survive and thrive regardless of the challenges it is facing (**collective efficacy**). Awareness and belief create **courage** to face organizational blockers and the complexity of the situation. The core also creates organizational **confidence** to access resources and discover new, practical possibilities. With research and examples, *Reinventing Resilience* makes a case that organizations can build resilience, create great workplaces, and help end the global workplace stress epidemic.

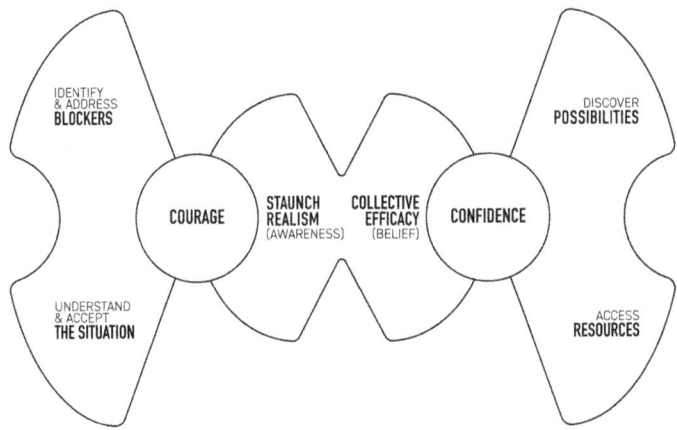

The Reinventing Resilience Model

MY FIRST GLIMPSE AT A WORKPLACE

My single mom worked hard to provide for my three siblings and me. She found a good paying job at Three Mile Island—the site of the worst nuclear disaster in the United States. (No, she doesn't glow). The job had great benefits and enabled her to support us. But the cost was high. I remember so many days when she'd come home tired and defeated not only from the job's physical demands but also from the horrible, misogynistic workplace environment her male counterparts created.

She was the only woman on her team. The men disrespected her and treated her as if she was stupid when they weren't socially isolating her. It was cruel, demeaning, and unbearably stressful.

And the shockwave of their behavior extended beyond her workplace and into our home. Her mood affected our moods. We knew there were times mom wanted to be alone, cry, or just get out of the house. We were afraid to ask, and she didn't want to dump her stuff on us. It was tense.

And, of course, the company did nothing about it. When my mom summoned the courage to speak to her manager or HR, they made it her problem. She felt trapped in her situation. She could not forfeit the income, yet she could not get help either. The implicit message was to bounce back… *every single day.*

I'm writing this book because I want to prevent that from happening to anyone ever again.

Why do we create workplaces that generate life-shortening stress when it is possible to create truly great workplaces where people thrive, and the organization gets the same results—maybe better results! We've got to do better.

STRESS AT WORK

For organizations today, the world is much like the Grand Canyon was for me: a vast, challenging landscape. Its beauty and potential are awesome, yet it can be ruthless. Organizations love to think at scale: quarters, years, decades. Yet they sometimes get tripped up by short-term, immediate challenges. And, like my challenging traverse across a vertical wall, organizations today constantly navigate difficult terrain with surprises at every turn.

Yet, as organizations hike through treacherous terrain, workers pay the price. According to Stanford professor Jeffrey Pfeffer, **workplace stress is the fifth-leading cause of death in the United States**—higher than Alzheimer's and kidney disease. In his book, *Dying for a Paycheck*, Pfeffer's research shows more than one hundred and twenty thousand deaths per year and 5 to 8 percent of annual health care costs may be attributable to how US companies manage their workforces.

Over a third of workers say their job or career is a regular source of stress. Among millennials and Gen Zers, the chronically work-stressed is 44 percent. Forty percent of all job turnover is due to stress (Hoel 2001). Healthcare expenditures are nearly 50 percent greater for workers who report high levels of stress, and job stress is the source of more health complaints than financial or family problems (NIOSH).

While organizations know workplace stress creates risk, lowers productivity, and stifles creativity and innovation, they have focused on *fixing* workers instead of the workplace. Many workers have access to various health and well-being remediation programs like mindfulness training, exercise programs, smoking cessation incentives, and flexible scheduling. But the implicit message is just bounce back. Just be resilient.

The actual problem is that organizations create conditions causing workers to tap into their deep reserves of resilience all day, every day.

Organizations are at a crossroads. Many are waking up to their workers' needs, but according to most C-level executives, the rate of change will only increase and put more performance and agility pressure on organizations. Big, disruptive challenges will come more frequently, and organizations that lack resilience are going to create more stress, not reduce it.

MY RESEARCH

This book draws upon my leadership experience (more on that below) as well as research and interviews with leaders across nonprofit, government, and private sector organizations. The organizations I studied include established global corporations, start-up tech companies, government agencies, fledgling nonprofits, businesses in transition, cross-sector community initiatives, countries experiencing growth and change, and even the world's oldest company.

I interviewed leaders from the YMCA of North America, Jay Peak Mountain Resort, All-American Entertainment, Protagonist Therapeutics, and Lippert Components to learn their unique perspectives on resilience and change. I also consulted with academics and researchers to help frame my thinking.

I drew upon examples from nature, the most resilient system available for us to study. I looked to the fascinating subterranean world of fungi as well as the planet's largest living organism for examples of what resilience looks like on a grand scale. I connect organizational resilience to natural ecosystems to put things in perspective, inspire action, and reframe our thinking.

This book focuses on reframing the idea of resilience to inspire organizations to act in new ways. I tell several celebratory and cautionary tales of organizations that have succeeded and failed to build resilient cultures. I'm confident you will see your own organization in these examples. It will inspire you to strengthen your organization's resilience instead of pushing for workers to carry the resilience load.

Reinventing Resilience builds on the work of so many researchers and thought leaders from David Cooperrider and Richard Boyatzis to Martin Seligman, Meg Wheatley, Karen Reivich, Melvin Smith, Ellen van Oosten, Tara Brach, Merlin Sheldrake, Jeffery Pfeffer, April Rinne, and others. I have drawn upon their findings and built on their insights.

WHAT'S IN IT FOR YOU?

I wrote this book for people who have a nagging feeling that organizations—no matter how well-intentioned—need to become better so the workers within them can become better. It's for those who want to build a case that organizations can and should change because the *status quo* is not sustainable. Internal change agents, managers, and senior leaders will have a guidebook that helps organizations get *unstuck*, much like Adam did for me in the Grand Canyon.

If you are responsible for organizational transformation, you may be interested in the *Reinventing Resilience* framework. It can help you convey to stakeholders the need to act at a systemic level. Similarly, the *reinventing resilience* model supports a case that organizations can develop organizational resilience. I believe the model can make reorganization, acquisition, rapid growth, enterprise-wide policy or tech changes, culture initiatives, or new behavior expectations much easier to implement and safer for workers' well-being.

While every organization takes its own path, every organization runs the risk of getting stuck when things become challenging. Instead of seeing those moments as *setbacks* that stop you in your tracks, you can keep going with courage and confidence to grow through the challenge. The *Reinventing Resilience* model will guide you.

WHY ME?

Guides are important on any journey. And you would be right in wanting to know what kind of guide I am. Who is Paul Thallner?

I'm a principal and member of the global leadership team at Daggerwing Group, a top-ten change management consulting firm. In that role, I provide strategic guidance to Fortune 100 organizations undergoing significant change and transformation. I lead amazingly smart and talented consulting teams who work shoulder to shoulder with clients to help them do change right the first time.

Previously, I've been an organization's president, a board member, a consulting firm partner, an executive advisor and coach, and a teacher for more than twenty-five years. I have worked in the nonprofit, government, and corporate sectors on projects ranging from statewide public policy, local education reform, organizational transformation, and institutional culture change. I helped build transformational change programs to end corruption in a province in South Africa and modernize the education system in Qatar.

Throughout my career, I have advised and consulted in some of the most interesting and challenging workplace environments—from hyper-growth tech start-ups to cash-strapped nonprofits. From massive corporate mergers to wildly dispersed and autonomous organizations. From globally intercultural companies to insular regional businesses.

On the academic side, I learned from the world's top organizational behavior researchers and faculty at Case Western Reserve University like Richard Boyatzis, David Cooperrider, Ron Fry, David Kolb, Chris Laszlo, Harlow Cohen, and more. I have certifications in several organizational change models and am active in several professional learning communities.

Most importantly, I've spent countless hours sitting across the table from executives who desperately want their organizations to change but can't quite figure out how to make it happen. I've seen them struggle to try to fit conventional thinking into contemporary problems. They care, and they want to try.

However, I've also spent way too much time with executives who believe workplace stress is for the weak and unworthy. They want those workers out of their organizations because it's *bad for morale*. These hyper-controlling personalities are often surprised to learn how much damage they do to their organizations. They can learn, but it's a journey.

I'm sick of organizations that portray themselves as wonderful oases of workplace excellence but, in reality, are terrible workplaces full of stressed-out workers. It needs to change. I've seen great workplaces, and I've been privileged to work in some. I know it's possible, and I want more than anything for your organization to be resilient—so you and your workers don't have to carry as heavy a resilience burden yourselves.

Do teams, organizations, communities, or countries have what it takes to move forward? To be better than they were before? Sure, they can bounce back. But bounce back to what? It's frightening, and my calling is to guide organizations through the difficult valleys of change. Your organization has what it takes. It starts by letting yourself take a step forward.

CHAPTER ROAD MAP

CHAPTER 1: DEFINING RESILIENCE
Resilient individuals have certain qualities that enable them to survive challenges and grow because of them. The neuroscience of resilience illustrates that perceived threats constantly challenge us. The challenging world of work keeps our brains on high alert, and we must actively manage our responses to inputs. The research into resilience provides a scaffold on which to think about resilience at the organizational level.

CHAPTER 2: WE'RE DOING THIS WRONG
The questions we ask are fateful, and confirmation bias is real. When organizations constantly ask "what's wrong," we end up with long lists of problems to be solved. This can lead to an internal narrative that the organization is fundamentally broken and it's lucky to be surviving at all. It creates what I call

gap-closing cycles—endlessly seeking and solving of problems to get back to an elusive *normal* state. Resilient organizations, on the other hand, balance problems with possibilities. They add new and different questions to reframe the organization as capable of solving its problems. This breaks the gap-closing cycle and creates hope, optimism, and possibility.

CHAPTER 3: THE WORKPLACE STRESS EPIDEMIC
Workers are stressed out, and the impact of workplace stress on individuals, the people around them, and the economy is massive. Significant change will continue to happen, and it's likely to accelerate. This puts workers at greater risk for stress and its effects. Organizations tend to focus their interventions on the workers but not on the system that creates stress in the first place. Of course, workers need direct support, but organizations can also control the systems, structures, processes, and culture to reduce worker stress.

CHAPTER 4: HOW RESILIENCE SCALES
We tend to think of resilience as a soloist pursuit, but examples of resilient systems are all around us. From enduring organizations to ancient organisms, growth—not just survival—defines their resilience story. The case study of Jay Peak Mountain Resort illustrates how resilience scales from the individual to the organizational levels.

CHAPTER 5: THE LIFE-GIVING SOURCE OF RESILIENCE
Like the transitional point where river meets ocean, organizations exist in the space between sensing their environment

and responding to it. Resilient organizations have profound self-belief that they can thrive no matter what happens. They also have an uncanny ability to see their internal and external context with crystal clarity. I call these characteristics collective efficacy (belief) and staunch realism (awareness), and they are at the core of the reinventing resilience model. Together they nurture an organization's ability to build resilience capacity.

CHAPTER 6: COURAGE

Organizational courage is one of two components that emerge from the life-giving source of resilience—see above. Courage enables organizations to identify and address their blockers. It also helps organizations understand and accept the situation they are in. This chapter explores how to build organizational courage.

CHAPTER 7: CONFIDENCE

Organizational confidence also springs from the life-giving source of resilience. When organizations are confident, they have greater access to hidden resources. They also can create practical, inspiring possibilities to drive the organization forward. We explore how to build organizational confidence in this chapter.

CHAPTER 8: LIFE IN THE ESTUARY

When staunch realism and collective efficacy are flowing and in balance—like the brackish water of an estuary—the organization feeds its courage and confidence to grow through challenges. This chapter explores how various organizational types stack up against the reinventing resilience model and concludes which types are likely to thrive and which ones are heading toward extinction.

CHAPTER 9: DWELLING IN POSSIBILITY

Resilient organizations understand their journey will be full of ups and downs. They avoid spending too much time in the valleys, but while they are down there, they learn what they can before moving to higher ground. They take advantage of the vistas to scan the countryside and plan for their next challenge.

CHAPTER 10: CONCLUSION

Organizations have been sources of worker stress for far too long. While we can't eliminate stress from work, we can create resilient organizations that limit the amount of stress that permeates workers' lives. It is our calling to guide our organizations into and through difficult terrain. We must build organizational courage and confidence to grow through difficulties, not simply survive them.

∗ ∗ ∗

Scan the QR code below for more information and resources specific to the introduction.

CHAPTER 1
Defining Resilience

Over every mountain there is a path, although it may not be seen from the valley.

THEODORE ROETHKE—AMERICAN POET

OVERWHELM

Day after day, it was all ratcheting backward. In the summer of 2020, during the height of the pandemic, everything went from bad to worse to even worse. Just like what happened at the Grand Canyon, I apperceived all my life's challenges in a dizzying moment of awareness. The feeling of overwhelm was like an out-of-body experience.

My mom went through torturous oral surgery, and shortly after her discharge, she was back at the hospital with chest pain. My sister received a difficult medical diagnosis. My father-in-law was in continuous AFIB. We were grieving the loss of my stepfather, a brilliant, caring, and accomplished man. Friends were having similar experiences, which added to compassion fatigue and made it harder to access supportive resources.

Of course, at that time, the pandemic was shutting everything down. My clients started pushing projects out months or backing out altogether. My son was at home twenty-four seven because nobody was socializing, so I felt guilty he wasn't receiving a quality upbringing. At the same time, the political madness in Washington and the racial reckoning following the murder of George Floyd just magnified my belief the world was coming apart at the seams. Meaning was starting to feel elusive.

SAVING THE SKI INDUSTRY

Olivia Rowan, the publisher of *Ski Area Management Magazine* (SAM), had been a client and friend for years. On a call with her one day, I reflected out loud that if I felt this challenged, others were probably feeling overwhelmed, too. If the overwhelming feeling was hitting an entire industry at once, what would that mean for its long-term sustainability?

She immediately understood where the conversation was going, and we began to put a few pieces together. As a trade magazine publisher, she deeply understands the industry and has a massive network across the ski community. General managers would call her daily to share their struggles with constantly changing mandates, conflicting health information, widespread worker fear, and guest hostility. One message came through loud and clear from ski area leaders across the country, "We're in major react mode, and everyone's just hanging on by a thread." They knew there was no end in sight.

INDUSTRY HUDDLES

Helping these leaders and their employees was not an option. They were struggling, and Olivia and I, along with her team, brainstormed ways we could help. We immediately started monthly industry-wide Zoom huddles. They were a combination of sharing and learning sessions but also served to keep the struggling community intact. Typically, between two hundred to three hundred people would join the calls to hear the most respected leaders in the industry express their vulnerability and humility in the face of incredible challenges.

But the huddles were not enough. Many workers in the ski industry are seasonal, so the huddles weren't reaching everyone during the summer. Similarly, resorts were holding back on professional development spending and needed a low-cost solution that reached everyone. Whatever we created needed to be honest and practical, like the mountain culture itself. They like to hear it direct and straight—no fluffy stuff.

Olivia and I decided an online resilience course accessible to all and tailored to the specific needs of the mountain resort industry would be perfect. We could make an impact with Olivia's ability to communicate with the entire industry and my organizational change expertise. In September 2020, I started researching resilience, but with an eye toward helping an entire industry bounce back.

REDEFINING RESILIENCE

I dove in. I contacted Tanya James, a classmate from my Master of Organizational Development program at Case Western Reserve University. She is senior managing director of Positive Change and Development Pty Ltd., an Australian consultancy that helps organizations through complex transformational change. For the next few months, Tanya and I shaped the initial model we would use for the online course.

We started by defining resilience and soon discovered its nuanced and counterintuitive meaning. We often describe resilience as the ability to get back up when knocked down. Or the ability to bounce back from a setback. That's true. But it's a lot more complex than meets the eye.

It turns out we limit ourselves by thinking of resilience only when we experience a setback. While most people reflexively associate setbacks with resilience, when given a chance to think about it, they realize there's more to it than that.

I asked one thousand one hundred of my connections on LinkedIn to respond to a poll. How would you describe resilience? I gave them three choices: A) Like a sponge: bounces back to its original shape after being squeezed; B) Like a steel rod: strong enough to withstand bending pressure; or C) Like a garden: continually growing even when the weather is difficult. More than 80 percent of respondents chose C—like a garden.

Answers A and B are what we typically see in news headlines. Heroic organizational or athletic comeback stories are sponge examples. An organization that fights off a hostile takeover counts as a steel rod story. We get mixed messages about resilience. Is it strength? Or is it flexibility?

When given a choice, my network picked C—a garden. Thinking of resilience as a garden that continuously adapts to thrive shifts the popular narrative about resilience. The world reinforces the idea that it's about closing gaps, getting up, or powering through. Yet, many intuitively believe resilience is an affirmative, strengths-based quality one can cultivate.

EVOLUTION OF THE MODEL

Based on our independent work in organizations and deep training in organizational change theory, we began playing with the intersection of individual and organizational change. We concluded resilience is multifaceted.

Resilience involves the act of balancing the way we look at a situation with our understanding of what's in (and out of) our control. The more we confront what's happening, the more awareness we acquire about what may be possible.

That effort to make sense of the challenge tends to increase our sense of agency—our belief in our ability to navigate difficulty. With more agency, we can see more viable options. Tanya and I started thinking of resilience as a self-feeding virtuous cycle:

- Resilient people are very good at objectively looking at reality—this involves facing yourself and all your fears and triggers while facing the situation. This process builds your courage.

- Resilient people also believe the difficulty they're facing is temporary and—even though it might be tough—they'll get through it. They have self-belief and personal agency.

- Personal agency enables one to see possibilities, especially ones where the situation creates growth and strength.

- But resilient people tend to filter possibilities to those they can help create or shape in the future, not far-fetched fantasies that will never come true. They move in the direction of what they think is possible in the future by accessing their internal and external resources.

As resilience strengthens, it strengthens you as well. It's a choice to use the situation to grow. A lot of people *go through* challenges, and that's all. But many are also on track to *grow through* their challenges. The latter is much more resilient.

QUALITIES OF RESILIENT PEOPLE

Over the past twenty-five years, I interviewed, coached, consulted, and advised hundreds of senior-level leaders. I also interviewed dozens of executives, consultants, and academics for this book. I researched what makes people resilient and how top companies teach resilience to their most promising talent, and these are the top qualities of resilient individuals:

- **Believing in one's own ability—self-efficacy.** At their core, resilient people believe they can get through a challenge even if the way through it is difficult.

- **Seeing the context clearly and unflinchingly—staunch realism.** Resilient people don't tend to fool themselves or wear rose-colored glasses. They focus on facts, data, and truth while avoiding wishful thinking.

- **Understanding their fears and triggers.** Resilient people tend to have at least some awareness of their triggers, even if they can't name them. They can objectively see them and control their responses a bit better than most.

- **Accepting the situation.** Resilient people can see a situation for what it is, even if it is very painful to look at. They tend to stay "present" with the present.

- **Choosing from among a filtered set of reasonable possibilities.** When resilient people choose their way forward, they tend to pick from among several practical possibilities. They don't jump out of the frying pan and into the fire. Even if all the choices are poor, they pick one they can live with.

- **Accessing hidden resources.** Resilient people don't treat a challenge as if it's their first. They draw upon their full range of resources to help them move forward—even if those resources are hidden or infrequently accessed. For instance, we can forget or downplay our self-qualities, skills and knowledge, and social supports when we need them most.

NEUROSCIENCE OF RESILIENCE

In our study of resilience, we looked at the connection between stress and how people respond to challenges. That led us to the neuroscience of *triggers*.

I will use the word triggers to refer to things that set people off. That is, things that create an immediate, strong, and emotional response. Things you react to without even thinking about them. When encountered, triggers make it hard to make a rational decision. For many people, public speaking is a trigger. So is getting cutoff in traffic. Walking in the woods at night, hearing a floor squeak in your house when you're alone, or a big dog running toward you can be triggers as well. What about your phone ringing and seeing it's your boss? What about a demanding email in all caps? What about the looming deliverable deadline? What about being mansplained?

Resilient people have **courage** to recognize when they feel triggered and to face their triggered self. When we are triggered, our behavior tends to be regrettable or misaligned with our idea of who we are. Or it is out of sync with the way others expect us to be. So, facing the moments when we *aren't ourselves* or *not at our best* takes courage. Resilient people have developed strategies and approaches to acknowledge their triggers and respond well.

But how do triggers even work?

Have you ever yelled at anyone in traffic? Have you ever jumped out of your skin after seeing your shadow? If so, you may have experienced an *amygdala hijack*.

Daniel Goleman, the author of *Emotional Intelligence*, coined the term amygdala hijack to refer to an immediate and overwhelming emotional reaction that's disproportionate to the stimulus because it triggers a deeper emotional threat (Goleman 2020).

You may know the amygdala is a part of the brain responsible for your emotional reaction. But you may not know it's sensitive, always on guard, and can control other parts of your brain. That is, it can take over or stop other functions in your brain.

When the threat is mild or moderate, your rational brain can override the amygdala, enabling you to respond in the most rational, appropriate way. However, during a peak stress moment, the amygdala can shut off your neocortex, the front part of your brain responsible for reasoning, logic, critical thinking, conscious thoughts, and sensory perception. Your logic becomes overridden with emotion, and you're poised to simply act.

To understand why this happens, let's step into the way back machine. Animals' neurological systems prioritize survival: scan for threats, respond quickly, live to see another day. The fight, flight, and freeze responses evolved to improve the chances of survival. They are automatic responses to physical danger.

Early humans had the same neurological hardwiring. If a person saw a tiger, their amygdala was responsible for hijacking their neocortex, limiting all other thinking, and presenting a very limited number of options: fight, flee, or freeze. Those who survived a tiger encounter were likely the ones whose amygdala prioritized the flee response. Other responses like fight evolved to be used for more equally matched threats like another human. Freeze is a response that happens when fear floods our brains and we literally can't move. That is what happened to me at the Grand Canyon—complete paralysis.

The fight-flee-freeze response was appropriate for early humans because of threats, but the hardwiring remains part of us. Today, there are far fewer physical threats, but there are constant psychological threats caused by the pressures and stresses of modern life like angry customers, irate bosses, and slacking team members, or more broadly, economic uncertainty, geopolitical volatility, and global warming to name a few. These can impact our brain's ability to think rationally in the same way a menacing tiger did way back in the day.

When you feel threatened and afraid, the amygdala automatically activates the fight-flee-freeze response by sending out signals to release stress hormones like cortisol and adrenaline that prepare your body to fight, run away, or stay still. These hormones can remain in your body for four hours after a stressful incident.

According to the Mayo Clinic, health problems that can come from long-term activation of our stress response include: anxiety, depression, digestive problems, headaches, muscle tension and pain, heart disease, heart attack, high blood pressure and stroke, sleep problems, weight gain, and memory and concentration impairment.

TODAY'S WORKPLACE THREAT RESPONSE
Fight, flight, freeze. You've probably heard of these before. But there's one more response you might not have heard of: **appease**.

The appease response is meant to de-escalate a situation so that whoever or whatever is threatening makes another choice. It may have evolved in humans to survive the threat that lay within the tribe's primitive hierarchy.

But this response exists elsewhere in nature, too. There's a video on the internet of an encounter between a polar bear and a husky sled dog chained on his owner's property. When the bear approaches, the dog tries to play. He gets up, walks around, and uses his chain to move the bear around. Most people thought it was cute. But let's break it down.

The dog had few choices: He couldn't freeze since the bear spotted him and was even touching his head. He couldn't fight because the bear was much bigger and stronger. And he couldn't flee because he was chained up. His only option was to appease the bear by getting it to think of something other than eating him. Therefore, he did what he could to engage the bear in some other way.

Sound familiar? In our contemporary workplaces, this happens all the time. We can't freeze since our work is visible to our colleagues and supervisors. We can't fight because, well, there are laws against that. While a record number of people fled the workplace during the pandemic, we can't run from the reality we need money to survive in this world. When we become triggered at work, most of us use appease mode.

The amygdala hijack is a biological response that's supposed to turn on briefly, activate a response, and then go back to complete ease or what's called a *rest and digest* state where your body can do its main functioning uninterrupted. In primitive societies, violent encounters were periodic. People reacted in the moment, but those moments were somewhat infrequent.

THE INSIDIOUS AMYGDALA HIJACK

Today's *threats* are not necessarily hostile actions, but they're a lot more frequent: a deadline, a meeting with the boss, being asked to stay late, hearing a second-hand rumor about yourself, poorly delivered feedback, presenting, or working with that annoying colleague nobody likes. They register in our minds as threats, and we deflect or minimize them but never eliminate them. They loom in our minds creating a persistently stressed state and lowering the threshold for triggering events.

Mostly, we can rationalize life's threats. We understand that living comes with some risk, so under normal circumstances, we're not walking around in fight, flee, freeze, or appease mode every second of every day.

However, workplaces can erode our ability to manage our response. Small threats add up like straws on a camel's back. They can begin to accrue in our minds making us feel threatened, less secure, and more stressed out. They conspire to create a phenomenon researcher and professor Richard Boyatzis calls chronic stress. It is a condition where the accumulation of stressors has a corrosive effect on our ability to react and respond rationally to otherwise low-level threats.

For instance, getting an all-caps email from your boss doesn't usually justify slamming a laptop closed. But when the email arrives after a tense conversation with your teenager, a frustrating shopping experience at the grocery store, your low fuel light coming on, and your spouse not unloading the dishwasher, then that email can become a spark that lights the powder keg. You respond way out of proportion. *SLAM!* That's a modern amygdala hijack.

These hijacks can and do happen to everyone. When they do, they can cause us to question our resilience. Goleman, Boyatzis, and others have developed coaching and other strategies to help people build the capacity to manage and regulate their responses. People need to strengthen their emotional intelligence to function more effectively in organizations. And as we will see later in this book, organizations need to build resilience, so workers have fewer threats to respond to.

RESILIENCE INSIGHTS

Life gives us an opportunity to study stress at scale. While each day presents new challenges, they also give us a chance to examine patterns of behavior. In those patterns, we can see several promising qualities about ourselves as humans.

First, we're already resilient. Of course, we are. We wouldn't have made it this far if we weren't. Considering the history of humanity, it's fair to say people can not only survive but they can thrive.

Second, the definition of resilience we have been using is insufficient for our times. People do not have time to bounce back from one *setback* before getting hit with another... and another and another. It's got to be about more than getting up. It must be about learning, growing, and ultimately thriving.

Third, resilience is a quality that can be strengthened by working to understand our mindsets, beliefs, behaviors, and triggers. Resilience itself is not a skill, but there are lots of skills to develop that will increase and improve one's resilience: Raising your awareness of your emotional responses to stress, for example, helps you see what can get you triggered. Building self-discipline around evaluating a situation for what it truly is and reducing wishful thinking helps create boundaries within which to develop realistic solutions.

CONCLUSION

The ski industry had its best year ever in 2021–22. It's the most resilient industry I know. But it's resilient *not only* because it's full of resilient people. It's full of resilient organizations like Jay Peak Mountain Resort, which has grown through numerous challenges from ownership turmoil to climate change. I discuss this more in chapter four. The industry proves that resilience scales.

We can't do resilience alone. My feeling of overwhelm during the pandemic tested my resilience, and I was metaphorically back in the Grand Canyon, frozen in fear. I was losing my grip. But just like in the Canyon, the Adams showed up. More importantly, I let them help. I stayed busy, visible, and in touch. I cultivated professional partnerships, participated in learning communities, hired a therapist, and spent more time with my wife and son.

It was like standing in the brackish water of an estuary—abundant life, death, noise, movement, diversity, and the feeling everyone was in the same situation. As overwhelming as it was, zooming out to see the reality of the situation from another perspective made the overwhelm feel less acute, personal, and final. I grew through the challenge because the supportive systems around me grew through theirs.

CHAPTER SUMMARY

- The origin of the organizational resilience model in this book comes from a deep dive into how individuals build resilience.

- The mountain resort industry has experimented with resilience at scale.

- Resilience is multifaceted, nuanced, and too complex to be boiled down to bouncing back.

- Resilient people have several strong qualities already, yet anyone can develop those qualities to increase resilience.

- Neuroscience gives us a framework for understanding our responses to different situations.

- Workplaces tend to keep people in a heightened state of alert, which lowers the set point for stress.

* * *

Scan the QR code below for more information and resources specific to this chapter.

CHAPTER 2

We're Doing This Wrong

The greatest danger in times of turbulence is not the turbulence—it is to act with yesterday's logic.

PETER DRUCKER

QUESTIONS ARE FATEFUL

"Why precisely are the kids failing?" That question set in motion a series of consequences that dehumanized students and those who worked hard to educate them.

Early in my career, I worked at a nonprofit organization whose mission was to help a collection of urban charter schools succeed. The organization defined school success as outperforming students from neighboring suburban districts on statewide standardized tests.

Our funding was tacitly dependent on the students' academic performance in these schools. If the students did well on standardized tests, it strengthened our argument that our services helped deliver that outcome. If not, our funders would lose confidence and stop funding us. Our funders incentivized us to answer the question "why are the kids failing?"

The pressure to get the students to do well on the standardized test narrowed our focus to the point that we became essentially a test prep organization. Our job was to point out students' academic shortcomings so teachers could employ strategies to get students up to speed before the standardized test. Strategies included separating students by performance level, providing targeted instruction on the discrete areas of low performance, one-on-one tutoring, after school programs, worksheets, drills, and more. We somewhat euphemistically referred to all that as support.

The underlying and unspoken sentiment, however, was that the kids were *not enough*, and we had to fix them. We created a system based on students' deficits. And when the tests came back with red numbers, teachers were made to believe *they* were not enough, too.

Teachers, to their credit, would try to add context to the student stories by telling us about their home life or other special circumstances that might impact their scores. Ultimately, teachers were judged by the scores, not their ability to teach nor their advocacy for kids.

I often wonder what would have happened if we had asked, "What's the greatest strength each student has?"

PROBLEM-SOLVING IN ORGANIZATIONS

Organizations move in the direction of the questions they ask themselves. If they ask "what's wrong," they will find examples of what's wrong. While studying organizational change at Case Western Reserve University, I learned a powerful example of how our collective thinking affects outcomes. It's a classic case study known to many organizational change practitioners. British Airways was having problems at their new flagship terminal at Heathrow airport. Passengers were not getting their luggage in a timely way upon arrival, and in some cases, bags were lost. It became a costly and embarrassing problem.

Using the organizational behavior principles of Professor David Cooperrider, a group of airline employees chose to reframe the question from, "How do we fix the broken baggage system?" to "How might we create *an outstanding arrival experience* for customers?" Changing the question shifted everyone's thinking and focused their attention on what good looks like instead of what *less bad* looks like (Lewis 2004).

The airline stopped thinking in terms of its deficits—all the problems related to baggage handling—and focused on its assets and strengths of hospitality, brand loyalty, cross-functional expertise, etc. This helped the airline reimagine new possibilities for the entire customer experience that went far beyond fixing conveyor belts, including a seamless reunion of passenger and bag. The airline put the customer at the center of the change effort, not the baggage handling system. As a result, it redesigned signage, employee roles, uniforms, lost bag protocols, and innovative new ways to get bags from plane to passenger.

The key to the airline's success was not its ability to solve problems but rather its ability to let go of the way they typically solved problems. It flipped from a deficit approach to a strength-based approach. It widened the aperture and went from focusing on gears and wires of the baggage handling system to a smiling customer walking through the terminal with a rolling bag. Once the airline looked at the challenge from another perspective—in this case, the customer—things began to change.

GAP CLOSING CYCLES

Deficit thinking is self-limiting. If all we do is close the gap between what's broken and what's *normal*, there's no forward progress. We end up in an endless and exhausting gap-closing cycle. Our minds become attuned to *what's wrong*, and we build long lists of problems to be solved. The desired future state becomes harder and harder to see as our myopia takes over. And as organizations plod along fixing problem after problem, they become numb to the idea that excellence is possible. It's all just one huge vat of problems; we'll never be good enough.

In my charter school example, we were trapped in a gap-closing cycle. We saw students, teachers, and even their schools as a set of problems to be solved. There was no presumption of excellence; no acknowledgment the students were whole, unbroken, and fine as they were; and no credit given to teachers for caring about the students as people.

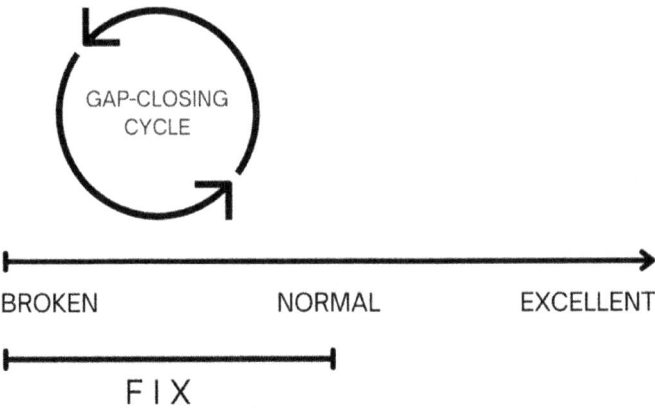

The gap-closing cycle, adapted from a lecture from Dr. Ron Fry.

The British Airways example, on the other hand, rejected that paradigm and broke out of the gap-closing cycle. It's a powerful and tangible reminder of how easy it is to fall into the familiar pattern of problem-solving. When organizations change the questions they ask, they change the direction they take.

IN LIEU OF FIXING

We are so accustomed to finding problems and fixing them that it's difficult for many to even think of a different approach to organizational change. Consultants often try to help organizations by conducting a needs assessment that identifies problems and focuses on what needs to be improved. This perspective reinforces the idea that the problem should be the focus of inquiry.

By focusing on the problem, individuals can fall victim to confirmation bias where all they see are more problems or deficits. They are blind to positive factors, and a negative spiral perpetuates a narrative that the organization is dysfunctional and full of unsolvable problems. When workers buy into the negative narrative, it sucks the momentum for positive change out of the organization and brings change to a halt.

What's an alternative? Dr. Cooperrider is a pioneer in the field of organizational change and developed a change model called Appreciative Inquiry (AI). AI is a method for creating systemic change through reframing questions, focusing on accrued organizational strengths, and leveraging the collective learning of the members of the organization's ecosystem.

Five principles form the basis of Appreciative Inquiry, and they are critical in understanding how resilience can scale from the individual to the organization (Cooperrider, 1999):

- **Constructionist Principle**—This is often restated in laymen's terms as, *words create worlds*. Reality is largely a subjective as opposed to an objective construct. What an organization *is* is interpreted by workers through the language they hear (both formally and informally). This is how some organizations can become set in their ways. They have built a reality in their collective minds that *it's got to be this way*. Habitual styles of thought, assumptions, rules, and other habits end up constraining the imagination.

- **Simultaneity Principle**—The shorthand for this is *inquiry creates change*. The moment we ask a question, change starts happening. Inquiry and change are not separate. Makes sense. If we start asking questions, the assumption is there's a disconnect between how you think something should be and how you are observing it. "Why are we falling short on production?" "Why is our turnover rate so high?" The moment you ask those questions, you plant seeds of change, discover new things about the organization, and start moving toward a different future vision.

- **Anticipatory Principle**—*Images inspire action.* The image workers have about the future of their organization influences their current behavior. If the image of the future is positive, then behaviors in the present will be more positive. Many organizations, to their credit, are focusing on becoming purpose-driven organizations. This gives workers a sense the organizational end game is more than quarter-over-quarter profit, which, in turn, helps them to feel that they are contributing to something greater.

- **Poetic Principle**—*We can choose what we inquire about.* Teams and organizations are like open books and are endless sources of study and learning. And, like a book or a good poem, they are subject to endless interpretation and inspiration. We have a choice in what to study in an organization. We can study the endless gap-closing cycles, or we can study collective sources of resilience. We could study all the crazy bureaucratic nonsense that slows us down, or we can study and amplify those moments of innovation that helped us accelerate. Either way, we have a choice in what to study in organizations.

- **Positive Principle**—*Positive questions lead to positive change.* Momentum for change, according to Cooperrider, requires large amounts of positive affect and social bonding. Momentum generates best through positive questions that amplify the positive core of the organization. Think of it this way, which question would you have more energy and enthusiasm to answer: "Where are all the places our process breaks down?" or "How might we become the easiest business in the industry to work with?" The more positive the questions you ask, the more energy and momentum you build. It's not avoiding problems; it's reframing them so we can see possibilities.

All this connects to resilience in an interesting way. If we ask, "What knocked you down?" "What set you back?" "What went wrong?" we end up pointed in the wrong direction. Those questions keep the mind focused on the problems, missed opportunities, deficits, gaps, and shortcomings. But they also focus on the past—which we cannot change.

BREAKING FREE FROM GAP-CLOSING CYCLES

Ron Suskind's 1999 book *A Hope in the Unseen* tells the story of Cedric Jennings, a high-achieving student from southeast Washington, DC, who—despite significant systemic, social, and financial obstacles—gets accepted to Brown University and suffers severe culture shock. While it's a heroic tale for Cedric, it exposes calcified systems built on gap-closing mindsets.

At Ballou Senior High, a violent inner-city school in Washington, DC, bright students had learned to keep a low profile to avoid becoming targets. Cedric Jennings was the brightest among the bright, and he knew his intellect could create an end to the cycle of poverty his family had been in for several generations. However, he lived in what some have characterized as a bucket of crabs. Everyone wanted a way out. But getting out meant climbing over each other and pulling others down to escape.

During the summer of his junior year in high school, he received acceptance into a program at the Massachusetts Institute of Technology (MIT) for promising minority students. The program offered a glimpse into the possibilities and challenges not only of life outside his neighborhood but also of life inside a world-class academic environment. Ostensibly, the program enabled MIT to preview promising students and extend invitations to attend the prestigious school. At the end of the program, MIT decided Jennings was not enough. He did not receive an invitation to apply to attend MIT as an undergraduate.

Undeterred, he was accepted into and attended Brown University, an Ivy League school. Once there, he discovered that his high school honors program did not prepare him for the academic demands. His classmates knew so much more, and Cedric was continuously playing catch-up. Furthermore, he had very little in common with the students—many of whom came from privileged backgrounds. While the school accepted him, he didn't feel accepted.

Stories like this underscore how deficit thinking keeps organizations from growing. Inner-city public education systems and Ivy League schools use data to evaluate students against their definition of success. They chose to see Cedric's academic achievements—not him as a person. Therefore, the structures and systems ended up forcing Cedric into a *just bounce back* cycle.

Cedric's self-efficacy—cultivated and strengthened over the years by his mom—altered his trajectory. He rejected the prevailing self-limiting belief of hopelessness and decided to pursue academics despite the social risks it presented. He chose to frame his challenge more positively by asking, "Why not me?"

What if the district or the university had a mindset like Cedric's? What if they asked, "How might we create a welcoming and supportive environment for all students regardless of their futures?"

KILLING PYGMALION

In *Metamorphosis*, Ovid tells the story of Pygmalion, a sculptor who falls in love with a statue he made. Praying to Aphrodite, Pygmalion wishes for a bride as perfect as his statue. He gets his wish, the statue comes to life, and they get married (Ovid 1993). This trope appears over and over throughout the centuries as a lesson in wishful thinking. If you regard something in a certain way, it turns into the thing you think it is. These stories persist in the canon because they tap into something we all know is true. Our perceptions of people influence how we treat them.

Jean-François Manzoni and Jean-Louis Barsoux wrote about the opposite of the Pygmalion Effect in a 1998 *Harvard Business Review* article. They called it the Set-Up-To-Fail Syndrome. The syndrome starts when a worker misses a deadline, falls short of a goal, or otherwise fails to meet expectations. The worker's boss then tries to fix the problem by focusing attention on that person: watching more closely, requiring more oversight/double-checking, and providing more feedback. The worker feels a lack of trust and confidence in their own work and, eventually, begins to doubt their effectiveness and worth to the organization. They withdraw, and the boss sees the behavior as proof that the worker was a poor performer all along (Manzoni 1998).

A former colleague of mine was in a similar situation. We'll call her Melissa. She was a consultant with tenacious drive, massive intellectual capacity, and a straight-talking style that clients really appreciated and admired. She exceeded her billable hour requirement and continuously sought to bring in new business. She was frequently a go-to resource for writing high-stakes proposals or designing strategic interventions. She made a ton of money for the company.

However, her boss saw her in a different light. Melissa was ambitious, outspoken, and not interested in playing the internal politics game. Melissa frequently challenged the boss with her tough, direct questions, and the boss felt threatened. She set out to de-motivate Melissa with mindless make-work assignments, overly picky performance reviews, giving credit for her work to others, withholding bonuses, and ignoring positive client feedback. But to her credit, Melissa refused to live down to her boss's lowered expectations. Therefore, each day was an exhausting uphill fight to prove herself. Melissa eventually had enough and decided to leave.

The way bosses perceive workers has a profound impact on them. Do the Melissas and Cedric Jennings of the world tap into their resilience during moments like these? Yes! But they don't get caught in gap-closing cycles even when those around them live in that paradigm. They eschew setbacks, keep moving forward, and don't regard themselves as *needing to be fixed* no matter what others may think.

WE CAN DO IT RIGHT

The starting point for change is usually identifying something that's wrong, different, or broken. That's just how our brains work. The wisdom comes from knowing how to reframe a situation to deliver surprisingly good results. For British Airways, it was no secret that something was terribly wrong, and there was enormous pressure to make it right. Asking positive questions did not ignore the problem, but rather it liberated workers from the thinking trap of seeing nothing but problems.

Cedric Jennings and my former colleague Melissa faced tremendous external pressure to buy into the gap-closing cycle. The way others thought of them could have dramatically altered their trajectory. And for Cedric, the consequences were life or death. Fortunately, they rejected those pressures even though it was painful, difficult, and involved sacrifice. Their self-efficacy was stronger than the negative narrative they were hearing on the daily.

Ultimately the nonprofit education organization I worked for—the one based on "Why are kids failing?"—closed before fulfilling its promise to accelerate opportunity for economically disadvantaged kids. The organization's gap-closing mindset created an environment of judgment, shame, and fear. Principals and teachers had to focus on student shortcomings when their instinct was to focus on amplifying student strengths. Teacher turnover was high, and parent satisfaction was low in the schools we served. In the end, our questions proved fateful. We asked why kids were failing, and we ended up fixated on finding answers.

CHAPTER SUMMARY

- We tend to think of resilience as a gap-closing activity, and this ends up keeping us in a cycle of fixing instead of a cycle of growing.

- Gap-closing thinking is self-limiting.

- The moment we ask a question, we begin to create a change. "The questions we ask are fateful."

- Teams and organizations, like open books, are endless sources of study and learning. What we choose to study makes a difference. It describes—even creates—the world as we know it.

* * *

Scan the QR code below for more information and resources specific to this chapter.

CHAPTER 3
The Workplace Stress Epidemic

Hier gaan over het tij
de maan de wind en wij

INSCRIPTION ON THE OOSTERSCHELDEKERING STORM BARRIER. TRANSLATES TO "HERE THE TIDE IS RULED BY THE MOON, THE WIND, AND US."

THE GALES

Since 2013, cyclists and masochists have participated in the Dutch Headwind Cycling Championship. It's an individual time trial where riders pedal directly into gale-force winds. It takes place near the North Sea along the Oosterscheldekering storm barrier, but only in the fall or winter when the severe storms make the race possible.

"The course is eight and a half brutal kilometers. It's a serious event," said race organizer Robrecht Stoekenbroek. "We have a limit of three hundred participants. All the bikes are the same: no gears and just an ordinary brake... it's a typical Dutch bike."

Up to 90 percent of the drag on a cyclist comes from air resistance. That is, in calm conditions simply moving forward on a bike creates drag. When headwinds come into play, the amount of effort required to push through the wind magnifies substantially. According to amateur cyclist Ed Reeve's experiment for *The Draft* cycling blog, for each 5 km/h of additional headwind, a cyclist can expect to lose 10 percent of speed—assuming their power output is consistent.

Finishers glow with renewed possibility, having summoned the courage and confidence not just to wear lycra in public but to ride a bike through a mild hurricane. They chose this challenge, and they overcame it.

But the race also is a metaphor for reinventing resilience. The very act of moving forward creates some resistance, and we can persevere through it. But when the headwinds blow and create even more drag, we try to pedal faster. What kind of workplaces requires us to pedal harder into strong headwinds? And what is the effect on us?

SETBACKS

We can't talk about resilience without talking about setbacks. Earlier I talked about gap-closing cycles and flawed thinking about resilience. If we only close the gaps, the best we can do is end up where we *got knocked down*.

Not only do setbacks evoke a deficit-based framework, but they also ignore the reality that time and life continue to move on. The idea of getting knocked down to the point of stopping, or the notion of being knocked back to the point of needing to claw your way back to where you were, are ultimately mindsets that keep us from thinking about the rest of the context around us and the positive possibilities before us.

Of course, setbacks are real. The intent of this book is not to minimize trauma or suffering in any way. If an experience has you reeling to the point of being unable to function effectively in your world, please seek help from a qualified professional.

This book is a thought experiment on rethinking organizational resilience from a positive, strengths-based perspective. I want companies to consider setbacks in a different way, think about how they are impacting workers' lives, and truly believe that growth—not merely survival—is possible.

BEING AERO

Ultimately, I want organizations to be more aerodynamic so they shield workers from ferocious headwinds. Weekend cyclists and professional racers spend a lot of time thinking about cutting through the wind, reducing drag, and improving the average bike speed. I view resilience like being on a bike. Headwinds are part of the experience of riding; nobody can avoid them.

Sometimes organizations or teams find themselves on the Oosterscheldekering trying to ride into gale-force winds. Even then, the winds don't push the organization backward. The organization can keep moving forward by tucking into a more aerodynamic position, switching gears, and pedaling a bit faster. While that part may be grueling, the company becomes different and better from having experienced the gales.

If cycling is a metaphor for life, we're always moving forward. Sometimes fast, sometimes slowly. Headwinds come and push against our progress, and we respond. Having the courage and confidence not just to endure, but to grow from that experience, is the promise of reinvented resilience.

CHANGE AND BURNOUT

Change has been killing us for a while now. Back in 1869, an American neurologist named George Miller Beard observed the fast pace of mid-nineteenth-century life was taking its toll on people. Some patients were experiencing debilitating mental and physical fatigue because their world was changing so fast. Neurasthenia, literally *nerve weakness,* was a disorder of an overly taxed nervous system trying but failing to keep up with modernity. Symptoms included exhaustion, anxiety, despair, insomnia, palpitations, indigestion, and migraines. What he observed is today called burnout (Schaufeli 2017).

For years now, consulting firm Gallup has been tracking employee engagement in workplaces around the world. While most organizations focus on the low percentage of engaged workers Gallup reports, the firm also tracks *actively disengaged* workers as well. These particularly troubled workers are having a miserable work experience and spreading their unhappiness to their colleagues. The percentage of the global workforce that's actively disengaged has remained steady at 15–20 percent for over two decades (Gallup 2022).

More recently, the World Health Organization (WHO) acknowledged burnout as a global epidemic. They defined it as a syndrome resulting from "chronic workplace stress that has not been successfully managed." WHO also says burnout is characterized by feelings of energy depletion or exhaustion, increased mental distance from one's job, feelings of negativism or cynicism related to one's job, and reduced professional efficacy. (World Health Organization 2022)

Even before the tumult of 2020, roughly two-thirds of full-time workers reported feeling burned out at work at least sometimes. In a separate Gallup survey conducted in 2022, Americans reported the lowest levels of well-being since Gallup started studying the topic nearly two decades ago (Gallup 2022).

Data collected during the pandemic of 2020–2022 shows stress and burnout increased:

- Seventy-five percent of workers have experienced burnout, with 40 percent saying they've experienced burnout specifically during the pandemic (FlexJobs 2022).

- Sixty-seven percent of all workers believe burnout has worsened over the course of the pandemic (Indeed 2021).

- Thirty-six percent of workers said their organization isn't doing anything to help with employee burnout (Jezior 2020).

- Thirty-seven percent of respondents say they are currently working longer hours than usual since the pandemic started (FlexJobs 2022).

- Sixty-one percent of remote workers and 53 percent of on-site workers now find it *more* difficult to "unplug" from work during off-hours (Indeed 2021).

The risk of burnout is high, and as stress mounts, more workers are approaching their limits. Stress can lead to not only low levels of engagement but also diminished productivity across the enterprise, limited ability to innovate, and increased risk of poor decision-making. Among workers:

- Seventy percent are stressed about their health, jobs, and finances, and more than 20 percent spend at least five hours each week thinking about these stressors during their working hours, according to a Colonial Life study (Business Wire 2022).

- Forty-one percent of workers in the same study felt less productive when stressed, 33 percent felt less engaged, and 15 percent said stress made them look for a new job.

Partly as a result, in summer 2020, we saw a mass exodus from the workplace as the *great resignation* gained momentum.

STRONGER STORMS
VUCA (Volatility Uncertainty Complexity Ambiguity) is an acronym coined in the 1980s to describe the experience of soldiers on the battlefield. Nearly a century earlier, Prussian military commander Helmuth von Moltke said, "No plan of operations reaches with any certainty beyond the first encounter with the enemy's main force." This is often shortened to the familiar quote, "No plan survives first contact with the enemy." Military thinking is that if soldiers understand and train for the inevitable chaotic battlefield environment, they're more likely to figure out solutions to both survive and achieve their military objectives.

The business world has adopted VUCA since that time to explain the need for adaptability, innovation, and many other change concepts. It has been a convenient term to help organizations cope with the breakneck pace of change. In the 1980s, we were still using pay phones, faxes, and postage stamps. Not only would those soon become irrelevant, but the entire rulebook of how, when, and where work gets done would be completely rewritten.

MORE CHANGE

Would George Miller Beard be blown away by today's world? The amount change since his time is dramatic. But it's also inevitable. If you have ever spoken to someone in their seventies or eighties, they can bemoan the world as it's become. The world is different from the point when they understood and could master it. One day, we may be in our seventies or eighties saying the same thing. Everyone believes the world was simpler *back then*.

Instead of competing with the past, maybe it's time to recognize that change won't stop happening. Maybe the pace and volume of change are less important than its persistence. We can quibble about how difficult it is to manage our awareness of all the change going on, but there's no mistaking the fact that it will keep happening.

Change creates stress in our lives, teams, organizations, communities, and countries. When the stressors converge, we can find ourselves overwhelmed with feelings of desperation, loneliness, helplessness, or inadequacy. We can end up focused on a feeling of inevitable doom... that the only place for the world to go from here is, well, to Hell.

Workers today walk into our offices or log on from home with overwhelming feelings due to the constant sensation of change and uncertainty. That is, they're already stressed-out. When organizations fail to acknowledge the humanity of their workers, they compound their stress by forcing workers to either go it alone, as Melissa did, or find somewhere else to work.

THE PRICE OF ADAPTABILITY
Postpandemic evidence shows that the world has evolved and adapted in ways that people prefer. We must be getting better at change, right? For instance, about 20 percent of people worked remotely in 2019 (Owl Labs 2020). But since the pandemic, at least half of workers continue to work from home. Many deride CEOs that insist that workers return to the office as power-hungry boomers tethered to outmoded thinking.

Expectations of home delivery dramatically changed during the pandemic as companies quickly shifted to new ways to serve customers who no longer could come to their stores and restaurants. US e-commerce grew by 30 percent in 2020. "There will be some lasting impacts from the pandemic that will fundamentally change how people shop," said Cindy Liu, senior forecasting analyst at Insider Intelligence. "Many consumers have either shopped online for the first time or shopped in new categories (i.e., groceries). Both the increase in new users and frequency of purchasing will have a lasting impact on retail." (Insider Intelligence 2020)

We changed the world through our collective response to the pandemic. Yay us. Organizations can pat themselves on the back for having adapted during times of profound change, but do *workers* at those workplaces feel better now that they have proven they can handle a lot of change all at once? Many didn't stick around to celebrate their company's adaptability.

Several factors drove the Great Resignation, and burnout was among the most significant. According to Anthony Klotz, a professor of business administration and an associate professor of management at Texas A&M University, "There were lots of stories about frontline workers facing long hours and difficult conditions during the pandemic," he said. "There was burnout in parents, especially women caregivers who were juggling educating their children while working remotely, and there were reports of burnout in organizational leaders trying to manage through the pandemic. Burnout is a predictor of turnover: The way to deal with it is to get away from the source of the burnout. Some people needed a break, and many probably didn't have the ability to take a month or more off to take care of their mental health." (Barrons, 2022).

MINDFULNESS AND WORKPLACE STRESS

For those who stayed or found new roles, the workplace has become a surreal place that blends VUCA and Buddha. Workplace stress continues to soar as workers try to navigate the complexities accompanying dramatic change. Companies are responding by offering mindfulness and stress-reduction programs for burned-out workers.

Mindfulness has its roots in Buddhist and other ancient meditation practices. US scholar Jon Kabat-Zinn introduced mindfulness interventions in 1979 to treat stress and chronic pain patients while working at University of Massachusetts Medical School (UMM Health 2022). Since then, mindfulness has entered the workplace as a nonspiritual practice to help workers manage and mitigate workplace stress.

But we are over-relying on workers to build their own resilience and neglecting the work of building resilient organizations. Singapore-based consulting firm Sequoia Group understands the organization bears significant responsibility to create conditions for workers to thrive. The company uses the metaphor of the sequoia tree to illustrate that the forest giants may appear individually strong, but they rely on the interconnectedness of their roots to withstand the forces of nature. The forest's collective resilience strengthens the resilience of each tree. Its mission is to "create organizations worthy of people's commitment." This mindset helps their clients create enduring systemic change instead of settling for remediation programs.

Offering mindfulness and stress-reduction programs to workers is the right thing to do. However, I would warn organizations to be careful not to transfer their resilience burden onto workers. Doing so can perpetuate a destructive bounce back cycle. If we create resilient organizations using the model I propose in the next few chapters, we can liberate workers from the burden of excessive workplace stress and create an upward cycle of momentum, innovation, and organizational growth.

WHEN THE WIND HOWLS, BE DUTCH

A passage in the 1852 version of *The Sailors' Prayer Book: A Manual of Devotion for Sailors at Sea* read, "We may by care and skill be able to trim our ship, to steer our course, or to keep our reckoning; but we cannot control the winds, or subdue deceitful currents, or prevent disasters." Later, this was condensed to the adage we know today. "We can't control the wind, but we can adjust our sails."

People sign up for races like the Dutch Headwind Cycling Championships to test their strength. They understand the challenge they will face and elect to endure it. The wind is part of the appeal.

In organizations, however, the wind is often treated as a problem. We can't control the wind, however. Winds naturally buffet organizations and cause them to strain mightily against the pressure. If organizations looked forward to headwinds—like the hearty Dutch cycling competitors—they could more effectively focus on moving forward in an efficient aerodynamic position.

I see resilience as how well organizations slice through the wind that blows in their faces as they travel forward quarter after quarter. Forces are always acting on an organization, and many of them are uncontrollable. Resilient organizations have the collective awareness to see the weather for what it is while also the collective belief that they can navigate through it. The aerodynamic result reduces pressure on the organization and its workers—reducing burnout and enabling everyone to grow through change.

CHAPTER SUMMARY
- We have a global workplace stress epidemic.

- Change won't stop anytime soon, so burnout might get worse.

- Resilience is not about setbacks. It's about always moving forward.

- Organizations are providing short-term solutions in the form of stress-reduction programs.

- Resilient organizations relieve workers of some of the burden of being resilient on their own.

- When organizations make it easier to work there, stress will decline.

* * *

Scan the QR code below for more information and resources specific to this chapter.

CHAPTER 4
How Resilience Scales

For me, the song means many things. It's a song about alienation and loneliness. And yet the realization that all of us are in this situation makes us less lonely. That's the real message in a bottle. We need to behave as a world community, not just as separate countries or as separate individuals, but as one family.
STING. DISCUSSING HIS SONG 'MESSAGE IN A BOTTLE'

IT'S ALL ABOUT WE
Resilience can feel like a lonely, soloist pursuit. We tend to climb out of our personal valleys mostly through sheer will. When we think of our challenging experiences, we wonder if anyone can possibly relate to them. However, research shows that we tend not to talk about extraordinary experiences because we don't want to feel left out.

People live for social interaction, acceptance, belonging, and camaraderie. By sharing an extraordinary story, you are essentially saying, "Here's something we don't have in common. Want to hear about it?" There's social safety in discussing mundane examples of shared experiences but high risk in discussing more unique content. That is one reason it is hard to confide in a friend that you've lost your job or failed a class. We feel worse when we separate ourselves from the group (Khazan 2014).

The result is we suffer alone and focus our attention on our own struggles instead of those of our colleagues, teams, organizations, communities, or countries. We forget the person next to us is probably struggling with at least one major challenge in their life. We feel like castaways. Only rarely do we get a glimpse of our collective and shared struggles, like Sting describes when talking about his song, *Message in a Bottle.*

To advance as teams, organizations, communities, and countries we need to acknowledge the shared experience of struggling through the pandemic, war, or economic downturns. Shared pain brings us together, according to the American Psychological Association and other sources (APS 2014). Normalizing discussions around big challenges, herculean struggles, or strong headwinds enables organizations to thrive because they leverage our need for belonging, acknowledge the reality of the shared experience, and build stronger cohesion in our groups.

RESILIENCE SCALES

While the provenance of resilience is found in people, limiting our thinking constrains our ability to grow and thrive at scale. We can't settle for the idea an organization calculates its resilience by adding the resilience of its workers. When we do that, we perpetuate the soloist paradigm and create more isolation and greater disconnection within our organizations.

Furthermore, if resilience didn't scale, organizations would be unable to last beyond the founders, withstand turnover, or endure across generations. Case in point: Japanese construction company Kongō Gumi has been around since the year 578. Many resilient workers have come and gone, but it's one resilient organization.

PANDO

How do we get our heads around the idea of resilient organizations? After all, organizations are collections of people, each of whom is working through their own stuff. Yet, organizations have their own life cycles, their own personalities, their own purposes, and even their own souls.

Perhaps nature can point a direction. While researching organizational resilience for this book, I came across a story about Pando, the oldest and largest organism on Earth. It's about fourteen thousand years old, and it's probably seen a thing or two.

I was attracted to Pando—a 106-acre stand of Quaking Aspen trees in Utah—because of all the hiking I've done in the Adirondack Mountains of upstate New York. I've walked past countless trees: aspen, birch, beech, cherry, maple, oak, fir, pine, hemlock... you name it, I've seen it. I always assumed trees were solitary beings. They were the lucky survivors that out-competed other saplings in a slow-motion race skyward to reach the sun's rays.

But Pando completely changed how I look at nature—and organizations. It turns out Quaking Aspen trees tend to grow in groups called clonal colonies. They share not only a root network but also DNA which makes trees in the same network clones. Therefore, one clonal colony of Quaking Aspen trees is considered a single organism. Pando, in Latin, meaning *I spread*, is a huge clonal colony with an estimated biomass of six thousand metric tons.

It turns out that long-living networked organic structures are not that uncommon. Merlin Sheldrake, in his book *Entangled Life*, details the enthralling world of fungi. According to Sheldrake, fungi live a secret, connected, and sprawling life underground that enables them to move freely (albeit slowly) across the landscape. All living things, he argues, owe their continued existence to fungal processes that interact at the molecular level in the shallow, musky soils of the world.

Perhaps organizations are like Pando—full of individual trees with the same root structure. Makes sense. Each organization has its own mission, vision, and values that serve as core elements that guide everything from strategy to behavior. Yet, each worker, like each of Pando's trees, has a unique perspective of the organization, a different role to play, and their own contribution to the organization's survival.

Any one tree may be struggling to thrive, but the entire clonal colony has the capacity to sense and respond effectively to bigger challenges.

THE CASE: JAY PEAK MOUNTAIN RESORT

Okay. Nice metaphor, I know. But let's test the *reinventing resilience* model to see how it scales in a real human organization.

As we discussed earlier in the book, the ski industry has demonstrated resilience over the years and decades. Through land management and water rights challenges, global warming and other environmental threats, shifting consumer preferences, a high financial and physical barrier to entry, a reputation for elitism, and resort consolidation under centralized management, the industry has seen its share of change.

In a remote corner of Vermont called the Northeast Kingdom, the faces of Jay Peak resort employees adorn banners, placards, and posters across a sprawling campus. It's a brilliant, modern branding strategy that taps into consumers' affinity for conscious companies that respect their workers. However, it's way more than just a marketing campaign for tourists or an attempt to placate workers. The faces tell a deeper story of a resilient organization that meets challenges and grows through tough times.

Let's examine Jay Peak through the lens of the *reinventing resilience* model. Earlier, I described the core of the model as its source of energy: staunch realism and collective efficacy. In subsequent chapters, we'll break the entire resilience model down and share concrete ways your organization can become more resilient. For this example, we will walk through the case referencing the *reinventing resilience* model.

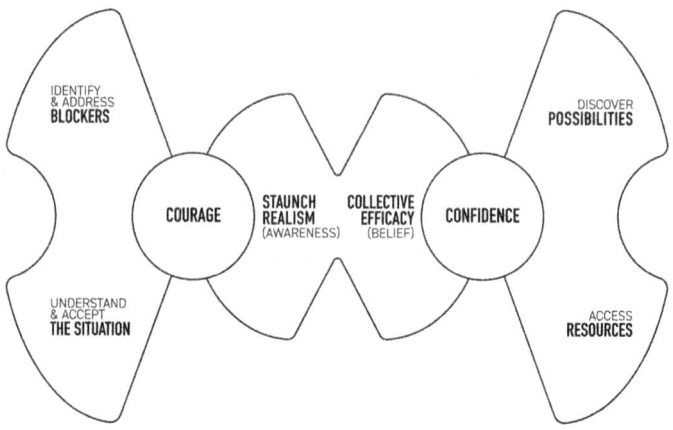

Jay Peak's resilience can be summarized with this model

THE SITUATION—NORMAL NO MORE

By 2016, the resort had been aggressively growing for about ten years. It added hundreds of hotel rooms, a golf course, new chair lifts, and other infrastructure to attract guests from the United States, Canada, and around the world to compete in the notoriously challenging ski industry. Other big projects like upgrading the high-speed tram to the peak to improve the skier experience were scheduled. The rapid growth was financed mainly by foreign investors leveraging the US government's EB-5 Immigrant Investment Visa Program. This program was designed to spur economic growth by allowing foreign investment in exchange for a speedier pathway to obtaining US residency status.

Murmurs of bad actors taking advantage of the program spawned national security and fraud concerns from Sen. Charles Grassley (R-IA), the Securities and Exchange Commission (SEC), and others. While there were many EB-5 fraud cases across the United States, the Jay Peak case ultimately became the most well-known.

On April 13th, 2016, at 12:40 p.m., Federal law enforcement agents arrived in black SUVs to suspend resort operations and investigate alleged fraud. Agents fanned out to the offices, told workers to step away from their computers, and began seizing records. Jay Peak's version of normal changed forever in the few minutes it took them to grab control.

THE BLOCKERS—ORGANIZATIONAL FIGHT, FLIGHT, FREEZE MODE

Steve Wright, Jay Peak's General Manager, talks in vivid detail about the afternoon of April 13th. The memories are forever embedded in his brain's neural pathways. One moment he was grousing about picking up his daughter's boyfriend and driving him to her track meet. The next moment, he had a federal agent poking a finger in his chest and telling him to go back inside, cancel his plans, and keep his hands where they could see them. After a cursory look at the organization chart, the agent said to Steve, "Which box are you?"

"I'm the Chief Marketing Officer," he replied.

The agent replied fatefully, "Okay, you're now in charge."

People react to threats—fight, flee, or freeze—when they believe they're in danger. When a threat happens at the organizational level the way it did at Jay Peak, collective fear of an unknown future can quickly lead to chaos. Steve and his team had to act fast to keep everyone confident about Jay Peak as a viable business.

They did that in two ways: first, they protected revenue any way they could. For example, Steve flew to Washington to rescue a booked one-thousand-person convention representing $1 million in revenue. He also spoke with dozens of brides and their families who had booked wedding receptions to let them know the resort would be there for their special days.

Second, he protected the resort's workers. As an executive, he had access to information about the investigation. But he understood the needs of those with no visibility into the situation: the lift attendants, folks working in the coffee shops, and even those in the Northeast Kingdom community. He knew workers would start freaking out if he stayed silent or operated in reactive mode.

His approach was to be transparent. "I wanted to get as much information out as widely and quickly as humanly possible and have it be as honest and transparent as the federal government will allow," Steve said. In doing this, he shone a light on the situation instead of avoiding it. This act of openness proved critical. He avoided a mass exodus, and a glimmer of hope remained.

RESOURCES—DEEPER THAN A VERMONT SNOWDRIFT
Resilient workers and organizations access resources they have at their disposal. Jay Peak's trusting culture is among its most valuable resources. Steve says Jay Peak's early days as a small resort full of friendly, loyal workers who genuinely

cared for each other created a solid foundation. He describes people there as having a "deep, deep, deep love of Jay."

"There's a generational love for Jay with employees and their kids and their kids' kids and grandparents, all working here," Steve shared. The previous general manager made it a point to be accessible to workers at all levels. He would clear tables in the dining areas, assist skiers onto lift chairs, and be visible and accessible to all. Today, Steve often does the same.

Many organizations facing major setbacks often feel helpless. Imagine the Federal government rolling in to take over your organization. You might feel overwhelmed and powerless to do much besides comply. Steve is the first to admit that was a tough moment. But he and the Jay Peak team soon moved beyond the initial shock, acknowledged the reality of the situation, and found something over which they had some agency: the people at Jay Peak. This helped workers suspend judgment during the SEC investigation long enough to see the creation of hope.

POSSIBILITIES—LANDING IN A NEW NORMAL

Jay Peak's setback could have ended in the resort's demise. But its collective resilience enabled it not only to survive but to grow through challenging times. Returning to "normal" was never going to happen, and in many respects, Jay Peak has leap-frogged its pre-EB5 state and transformed into a new, different, and better organization.

Ninety percent of brides decided to keep their wedding receptions at Jay Peak in 2016. And the wedding business has expanded since. The resort saw the completion of the major tram project, and skiers now have a faster and more comfortable ride to the summit. The conference business—once so important to survival—is thriving. Other improvements like a year-round water park, movie theater, indoor climbing wall, upgraded restaurants, a Nordic ski center, hockey rink, and summer mountain biking continuously attract local and traveling guests all year long.

JAY TODAY

Looking at the employees' faces on the banners, placards, and posters hanging in the indoor and outdoor common areas, we see the source of Jay Peak's resilience hiding in plain sight. Circumstances change, setbacks happen, and headwinds blow. Jay Peak has been able to meet its challenges because of the organizational and cultural strength it's built up over time. You cannot learn resilience in the moment. "There isn't any time for long thoughts when you're in [a difficult] moment," he said. "You're just responding to the hottest fire that's closest to your face."

Jay Peak and Pando continue to thrive despite new, bigger, and more frequent challenges. For Pando, a booming wild deer population, free from the threat of natural predators, snacks on Aspen saplings. Pando's new growth has slowed. Additionally, some fear environmental changes like global warming threaten the Aspen expanse and the dozens of unique species that call Pando home.

For Jay, environmental changes mean less natural snow, a shorter ski season, and higher operational costs. And a much more competitive workforce environment is making it very difficult for Jay and other ski resorts to attract and retain talented mountain resort employees.

RESILIENCE AT SCALE INSIGHTS

Regardless of the type of organization, there are a few observations I made while studying resilience:

All organizations face challenges. Every organization is unique, but there's nothing special about facing adversity. The ironic point of *Message in a Bottle* is that we tend to feel alone even when surrounded by others who feel the same way. It's common and natural for organizations (and workers inside them) to believe the challenges they face are unique and hard to describe.

Every big strong system starts as a small weak system. A series of early choices (or accidents) that keep the system alive make it strong enough to survive the next threat. Whether it is luck or skill, resilience builds over time. It's small at first, but it grows fast with every passing day. Resilience is the currency of survival.

Resilient systems are self-healing. You can damage part of a resilient system without disabling it completely. It can still function and thrive even while it is repairing itself. Resilient systems like Pando are protected by a different type of inner strength. Its strength comes from acquired and stockpiled reserves that enable it to thrive even if part of it is under attack.

Response and recovery time may vary. Humans can't perceive the speed of nature but living for fourteen thousand years is a long time by anyone's standards. Deer may be eating

Pando's saplings at a rate that threatens the ecosystem, but we have only been studying Pando since 1970—fifty years out of fourteen thousand. That's just .0035 percent of its lifetime. Just a blink of the eye. Pando survived many significant threats in its past, and we do not know if current threats are more challenging than what it's seen before. We must be careful to assess resilience with objective eyes since it's so easy for us to misperceive.

Resilient organizations rely on the same resilience framework as individuals. They have collective efficacy—a belief that they can grow through a challenge—combined with staunch realism—a knack for seeing the unvarnished truth and keeping their responses proportional to the challenge they're facing. They also know how to navigate the blockers that create a shared fight, flee, freeze response while also providing an honest appraisal of the situation. Finally, they tap into a deep well of resources (like experiences, history, or expertise) to help them imagine new, practical possibilities.

CHAPTER SUMMARY

- Resilience can feel lonely, but we're all experiencing challenges. The struggles may be different, but we share the experience of struggling.

- There are endless examples in history and nature of how resilience scales. Teams, companies, communities, and even countries can be collectively resilient.

- Jay Peak Mountain Resort experienced a shocking challenge. The way forward was not easy, but the resort's collective resilience enabled it to grow through its difficult moment.

- The *Reinventing Resilience* model is a useful framework for why and how an organization can grow and thrive in the face of extreme difficulty.

- Resilient organizations share certain characteristics that prepare them for moments that challenge them.

* * *

Scan the QR code below for more information and resources specific to this chapter.

CHAPTER 5
The Life-Giving Source of Resilience

One arrow can be easily broken. But, many arrows are indestructible.

GENGHIS KAHN

BUT MY PEOPLE ARE RESILIENT
Imagine picking up an arrow and holding an end in each hand. Applying pressure on the ends will bend the arrow. Makes sense. An arrow's shaft is deliberately flexible to account for the arrow launched from the same plane as the bow. Ironically, flexibility increases accuracy as the arrow *wobbles* through the air toward its target.

However, when you hold a bunch of arrows and try to bend them all at once, they barely move. They feel remarkably strong, almost as if they've lost their individuality and have a new identity as a strong, solid group of arrows.

This metaphor came up regularly as I thought about how resilience scales. I wondered if organizations were resilient the way a bunch of arrows are? That is, are organizations able to grow from challenges simply because there are lots of strong workers bunched together?

If that were true, resilience would linearly scale as organizations added workers. Larger organizations would be more resilient than smaller ones. Of course, we know that's not true in the real world. Many large organizations buckled under the weight of sudden or ongoing challenges: Blockbuster, Blackberry, MySpace, Radio Shack, Borders, Toys R Us, and internet icon Pets.com. More recently, the nation's oldest department store, JC Penny's, and other iconic retailers like Guitar Center, Nieman Marcus, Pier 1 Imports, and many more filed for bankruptcy.

These companies represent hundreds of thousands of workers, each with his or her own arrow-like strength, bundled together inside their corporate environments. However, organizations can be like a mess of arrows scattered across the floor. Organizations exist to organize people literally, so they all align. That is, they need to pick up the arrows, line them up, and point them in the same direction to create collective strength. Helping workers develop their own resilience is necessary but insufficient—you still could end up with a strewn pile of strong arrows. If people were tightly aligned like a bunch of Genghis Kahn's arrows, would JC Penney or Guitar Center's outcomes have been different?

THE PERNICIOUSNESS OF NARRATIVES

One reason companies fail during challenges is they simply don't believe they can win. They lack self-efficacy. In these companies, a narrative seeps in and lodges in the collective psyche. From the narrative, a new identity emerges. "We're old, outdated, slow, siloed, not innovative, not competitive, not strategic, or not nimble."

If you ventured into a Sears store during its decade-long liquidation saga, you would have seen the manifestation of low organizational self-belief. Once a mighty retail giant, its stores became hollow, lifeless storage areas for bygone brands. It's a case study in giving up as investors chopped up and sold assets instead of innovating for a brighter future.

In addition to giving up, failing companies can develop a warped sense of reality. Some believe they are still living in a prior era when success was easier. Or they blame other companies or circumstances for their failings. Fabricating a convenient reality might make senior leaders feel better, but it demonstrates an inability to see reality with a steely gaze; a lack of staunch realism.

Maybe staunch realism influenced decisions at Sears. They let go of nostalgia and recognized that competing against Wal-Mart and Target at the same time would lead to certain death. It's hard to believe when the reality is so hard to look at. That's why resilient organizations need BOTH staunch realism and collective efficacy to power their courage and confidence to grow through challenges.

THE ESTUARY OF RESILIENCE

An estuary is an area where a freshwater river or stream meets the ocean. Freshwater and seawater combine to form brackish water. Water continually flows into and out of an estuary—gravity moving the river's fresh water, and the ocean tides creating the flow of salt water. Some Native Americans called estuaries "Between Land" because they are not quite land and not quite water (NatGeo 2022).

The resilience model is also comprised of two forces joined together to create one ecosystem. Staunch realism and collective efficacy are at the center of organizational resilience, and in my model, they join to provide organizations with courage and confidence.

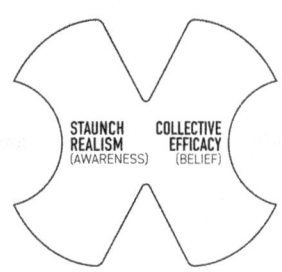

The engine of resilience

Collective efficacy is the shared belief by workers in an organization (or on a team, or in a community) that, regardless of the circumstances, the organization will not only survive, but likely thrive.

Staunch realism is the shared appreciation of the unvarnished truth pertaining to the circumstances an organization, team, or community is facing. Staunchly realistic organizations actively avoid fooling themselves with wishful thinking.

WHAT COLLECTIVE EFFICACY LOOKS LIKE

Hunger in the United States has been a problem for decades. Although our prosperity can blind us to the plight of the hungry, hunger's impact is profound. One in six children in America doesn't know where their next meal is coming from. The YMCA's hunger relief programs serve tens of thousands of healthy meals every day not only to kids, but to adults in every corner of America. Wherever you see a Y, there are hungry people nearby relying on it. Which means, that streetscapes in wealthy suburbs, rural villages, and urban neighborhoods... they all have hungry people.

According to Stacy McDaniel, Manager of Movement Engagement and Food Programs as well as the National Spokesperson for the YMCA of the USA, stories of hunger are everywhere:

- In Washington, DC where school closures cut off kids' food supply.

- In Minnesota where an upper-middle-class woman, who had never faced food insecurity before, had no awareness of the Y's safety net.

- In Florida where immigrant populations leverage the Y to help create community gardens.

Stacey and her team were met with a challenge that tested the collective-efficacy and staunch realism of the two hundred-year-old institution.

Food insecurity spiked in 2020 when the pandemic forced businesses and schools to shut down. Kids who were dependent on schools for their meals were suddenly cut-off as the world went virtual. Adults had to make up the difference while also navigating the blurry lines between home life and work life. On top of all that, resources the Y used, like restaurants, transportation networks, and suppliers were either closed or significantly constrained. The YMCA's own infrastructure felt the impact of the pandemic. COVID-19 mandates across the states forced YMCA chapters to shutter buildings and furlough workers.

While many would see this as a collective setback, Stacey and the YMCA team adopted a mindset aligned with the *reinventing resilience* model. They looked at the situation and chose to see possibility, not problems. The number of people needing food spiked, and the YMCA had to figure out how to adapt quickly to meet a sharply increased need with sharply reduced resources all within a volatile, uncertain, confusing, and ambiguous environment.

The YMCA started in 1840's London as a refuge for men who needed an escape from the chaotic streets of the day. Over the decades, the Y has scaled-up its capability to provide safe and healthy spaces for civil rights activists, immigrants, the economically disadvantaged, and others. It has a network of thousands of YMCA chapters and tens of thousands of staff and volunteers. The organization has been solving complex logistical problems to fulfill its mission for hundreds of years. By spending a lot of time preparing since its founding, the YMCA can tap into a core element of resilience: collective efficacy.

"This was our time," Stacey said. "While we could never have predicted the pandemic, we had the pieces in place. And this was it. This was 'go time' for us. We would never have wished for this, but it was a time to leverage all of that hard work we had done before and all of the relationship-building."

The Osage Prairie YMCA in Nevada, Missouri, exemplifies the collective efficacy of the organization. Nevada is a very rural community, and the YMCA there had just one full-time staffer. "... and I just want to emphasize... one guy!" Stacey said. The local schools closed due to COVID-19 and therefore could not offer kids meals. Summoning the Y's centuries of determination, he wouldn't take no for an answer. He saw possibilities where others saw problems.

He mobilized volunteers and partnered with the local grocery store. Volunteers helped register local citizens in need of food. The grocery store provided a truckload of food each week. Other volunteers handed out bundles of food every Saturday morning. The collective effort of the Osage Prairie community provided two thousand kids with a week's worth of food every Saturday morning.

Memphis, Tennessee, is one of the more impoverished communities in the YMCA network. Prior to the pandemic, the school district relied on a centralized commercial kitchen to feed more than one hundred ten thousand students across

214 schools. When the pandemic hit and the kitchen closed, they called the YMCA. Overnight, the Y stepped in to help tens of thousands of kids obtain meals. The creative and logistical effort was significant. The Y worked with the city of Memphis, which agreed to allow its workers and vans to help distribute the meals. Additionally, area churches and community centers in low-income communities stepped up to stage and store meals as well as hand them out.

The Monroe Family YMCA in Michigan told staff on a Friday that the schools would shut down. The Y served about one hundred kids in the after-school program, so they knew they had to pivot to continue serving them. Over the weekend, they brokered partnerships for church kitchens. They also obtained the use of the Lay-Z-Boy factory kitchen. They were able to scale up meal production so that by Monday, they could hand out one thousand meals.

Stacey says these successes resulted from devoted YMCA staff and volunteers as well as long-standing partnerships and strong community relationships.

Stacey framed the YMCA COVID-19 response as a wonderous example of decades-long preparation and confidence: "Did you ever think all of the work, all of the support systems, the connections, and the network we built was made for this moment?"

HOW TO LOSE COLLECTIVE EFFICACY

In the late 1990s, I worked at a Silicon Valley software company called Broadvision. It was the height of the dot com boom, and like most companies of that time, Broadvision wanted to convey power and confidence to woo top talent, investors, and customers. Like a peacock in full display, Broadvision had it all: a fancy headquarters building with all the trimmings, massive signing bonuses for tech wunderkinds, a whiz-bang product promising a lot, and even PR wins featuring the CEO on the cover of business magazines.

Like a lot of companies of that era, it believed in its own hype. Folks at Broadvision—me included—began to see reality through a very distorted lens. Our stock options made us all millionaires on paper. Big-name clients were calling us to help them build their global e-commerce solutions. Consultants like me traveled the world, had platinum elite status, and enjoyed conference rooms full of clients hanging on our every word. The stock price was soaring—outpacing everyone on NASDAQ but Cisco. We believed we were badass.

Broadvision lacked staunch realism to see that behind the hype, there were problems. The software we sold was complicated and expensive to implement, was full of undocumented features, also known as bugs, and was slower to evolve than that of our competitors. Also, the company grew from about six hundred when I joined to about twenty-two hundred two years later. The culture was straining against the growth as familiar ways of working either broke down or became systematized.

Without staunch realism, workers had little courage to call out organizational blockers. For example, when the company was smaller, some developers would be *in the zone* for long periods of time. They would sleep under their desks to save commute time. As the organization grew, the expectation that everyone was *all in* took hold. Overwork and burnout became the norm, and this blocker went unchallenged.

Over time, the confident, badass narrative shifted. Early signs of the dot-com bust started appearing as cracks formed in clients' online business models. Larger, more established clients grew impatient with project delays, less-than-perfect software, and team resourcing issues. Showy, expensive initiatives became awkwardly juxtaposed against client attrition, and the ever-elusive moment of becoming cash-flow positive. Our own workers weren't buying the swagger-fueled story anymore. They had lost faith; they didn't believe the company could win, and people started heading for the exits—me included.

In retrospect, Broadvision's loss of collective efficacy was like engines two, three, and four of a jumbo jet cutting out. The plane didn't quite crash, but it lost so much altitude the organization basically disappeared from the radar screen.

WHAT STAUNCH REALISM LOOKS LIKE
"If we're going to continue to see significant growth in our business and grow past $1 billion, we have to tackle our high turnover rate," Jason Lippert, CEO of Lippert Components, said one day in 2008.

The economic downturn during 2008–09 affected Lippert Components as it did many other companies. And even back then, high turnover was a costly expense. By asking themselves a simple question, "how do we reduce turnover," the maker of recreational vehicle (RV) parts and accessories chose a difficult path that led them to the truth and ultimately to growth through a monumental challenge.

Staunch realism is the ability to identify and accept reality even if it's painful to look at. Jason knew there was high turnover, but he suspected there was an underlying reality that he needed to see and understand if change was going to happen.

Jason recalled his thinking at the time. He knew the company could manage a turnover volume in the hundreds. However, if the company grew and the turnover rate stayed the same, thousands of workers would be coming and going each year. Not only is that costly financially, but it also makes creating and maintaining a strong culture nearly impossible.

The company also started rethinking its values around the same time, and he didn't want them "to just be stuck on the wall." He wanted a company that truly lived its values. Most companies struggle with a disconnect between stated values and lived values, but very few are brave enough to explore the valley that separates the two.

Jason and his team decided to go on a road trip to factories, warehouses, and showrooms across the country to simply ask workers what the company was doing well and not so well. It was a risky move since he did not know what he would find.

When given the opportunity for their voices to be heard, the employees spoke. They talked about the issues causing people to leave Lippert: lack of maintained facilities, poor relationships with management, lack of recognition, few career growth options, work-life imbalance, and the need for a clearer company vision.

For the first time, workers had direct access to the person who had ultimate decision-making authority. The flattened layers of hierarchy meant people were having human-to-human interactions. Issues were no longer transactions to be processed; they became real stories of what it was really like to work there.

Roles became less important, and people called each other by their first names. Workers at all levels sat comfortably, shed pretense, and told it like it was. It was the kind of conversation that only emerged when everyone felt safe and unjudged.

Jason created that safety by being there. He made an effort to meet people where they were. He spent time in their workspaces and viscerally felt what it was like to be in their shoes. This act of leadership humanized Lippert Components to his employees and opened the door to candid conversation.

He and his team treated the information they received with great respect. They confirmed or disconfirmed what they heard. They looked for patterns like a tracker looks for footprints in the wild. They included workers who rarely had their voices heard.

But mostly, he and his team worked hard to understand the points of view of those whose comments surprised them. A lot came out during those conversations, and it was important to let people get their thoughts out of their heads and into the room. Every idea, complaint, assumption, and solution were treated as valid.

Staunch realism takes work. The first step is being willing to take the first step. Jason allowed himself to believe that his reality might be different from that of his employees. And he decided to discover the truth within his own organization.

His approach was reminiscent of the US Navy SEALs *extreme ownership* philosophy. Extreme ownership means taking full responsibility for what is happening or what has happened. For example, SEAL leaders take responsibility if a subordinate doesn't understand instructions instead of blaming them for not getting it. Similarly, if a leader is not clear about instructions, it's her or his responsibility to go to superior officers for clarity.

Did it work? Rather than creating values at the central office and distributing posters to the manufacturing plants, distribution centers, and showrooms, Jason engaged in dialog. As a result, the company fixed facilities based on worker feedback, streamlined organizational structures to enable greater cross-functional collaboration and communication, and invested heavily in leadership coaching for the one thousand people-leaders at the company. By March of 2009, as the economy hit the floor, the company's stock was trading at $7.15 per share. It was brave at that time to adopt an extreme ownership mindset when it would have been completely understandable to adopt extreme cost-cutting. By late 2021, the company's share price was $160.26, annual revenues were $4.5 billion, and there were fifteen thousand team members globally.

HOW TO LOSE STAUNCH REALISM

There are two ways to lose staunch realism. The first way is by borrowing someone else's reality, and the second way is by getting others to tell you what reality is. Let me explain.

Early in my career, I was involved in public education reform. New laws made it possible to open semiautonomous schools—called charter schools—that could bypass some regulatory requirements in exchange for promising better results. There emerged a start-up culture where aspiring school founders would try their hand at building something new instead of trying to change the existing system from within. Lots of people were trying lots of things. Like tech and private sector start-ups, most failed spectacularly, some survived, and a few were considered unicorns.

Those that succeeded were studied. Founders and funders alike would embark on national tours to visit these academic oases to discover the *secret sauce*. The curriculum, the uniforms, the in-class routines, the rules, the parent and community involvement, and other features were all dissected to determine the extent to which they contributed to student performance on standardized and other tests.

Naturally, education entrepreneurs wanted to replicate these "winning" models. But many attempts to duplicate the shining examples failed. Why? It comes down to accurately identifying and accepting reality. The most successful schools were tailor-made for their specific environments and had cultivated not only systems and processes over time but they also had strong, aligned cultures engaged and committed to success.

Borrowing someone else's reality and dropping it into your own does not work. It's the same reason nobody could replicate Southwest Airlines' success for decades or why pro sports head coaches often fail in their second jobs after being successful in their prior one. Reality is cocreated, not copy and pasted.

The second way to lose staunch realism is by letting others tell you what reality is. A lot of CEOs in Jason Lippert's position would start with a forensic approach. Maybe they would hire a firm to conduct exit interviews or figure out which manager(s) are losing disproportionately more workers. They might analyze their wage data compared to that of their competitors. Or they may even consider if the "local talent pool" has been drained and it's time to move to a new city, state, or country.

There's nothing wrong with objective data, but the problem comes when we don't sufficiently consider the clients' reality. That is, discrete problem-solving won't explore the underside of the iceberg—the bulk of the problem that isn't immediately visible—the way Jason did. By owning the problem himself, he avoided a biased outside perspective and narrowed the gap between leader and worker, thereby tightening the organization's cultural cloth.

BRACKISH WATER OF RESILIENCE

Workers strengthen organizations. But organizational resilience is about much more than the aggregate of everyone's resilience. Companies, communities, and teams thrive when there's an abundant flow of collective efficacy and staunch realism. Like the estuary, they mix to create a unique, abundant, and resilient system.

Staunch realism gives organizations the courage to face reality—even if it's tough to look at. When they do, they tend to see their context more clearly and avoid impulsive reactionary decision-making. Collective efficacy gives organizations the confidence to access their full range of capabilities in response to whatever it's facing so new, better possibilities become more evident and reachable.

CHAPTER SUMMARY
- We need resilient people to make resilient companies. But organizational resilience is not simply the aggregate of each worker's resilience.

- Companies fail when people stop believing that success is possible and when leaders stop seeing reality for what it truly is.

- The source of organizational resilience is a live-giving estuary where collective efficacy and staunch realism come together.

- Collective efficacy is the shared belief by workers that, regardless of the circumstances, the organization will not only survive but likely thrive.

- Staunch realism is the shared appreciation of the unvarnished truth pertaining to the circumstances an organization is facing.

* * *

Scan the QR code below for more information and resources specific to this chapter.

CHAPTER 6
Courage

You gain strength, courage, and confidence by every experience in which you really stop to look fear in the face. You are able to say to yourself, 'I have lived through this horror. I can take the next thing that comes along.' You must do the thing you think you cannot do.

ELEANOR ROOSEVELT

Collective efficacy and staunch realism reside at the center of the reinventing resilience model. The model is shaped like a hummingbird's body: the center holds the wings and provides the strength to move them.

Courage is one of the two outputs that result from working on the resilience model's core. When organizations have a clear-eyed view of reality and collective self-belief, they tend to have a lot more courage to face challenging situations.

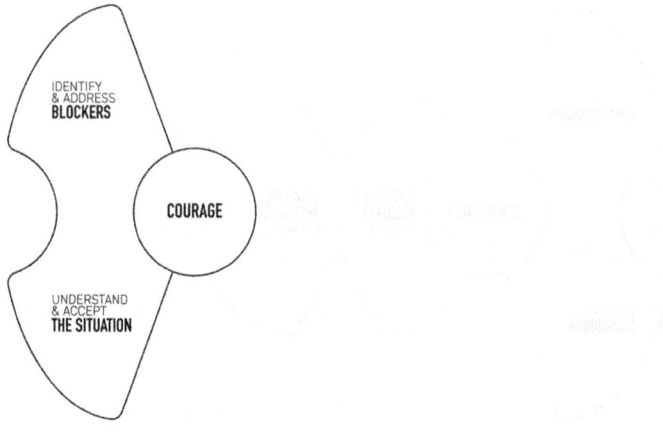

Resilient organizations have courage to face their blockers and the situation.

WHAT IS COURAGE?

Courage is the ability to face and deal with something even when we are afraid of it. Inside the brain, we often have deeply conflicting responses to our life experiences. Why? Humans are hardwired to avoid or run from scary things. But we also have a rational mind that is curious and wants to learn about the unknown and unfamiliar. Courage is how I describe the intentional act of moving a response from the primal brain up to the rational brain.

At the organizational level, this plays out in several ways. Organizations face frightening things all the time: strong competitors, quickly evolving technologies, economic downturns, political unrest, policy shifts, employee upheaval, and even pandemics. And depending on what's scaring it, an organization can respond the same way people do: running, fighting, avoiding, getting stuck, or giving up.

HOW TO BUILD ORGANIZATIONAL COURAGE
Building organizational courage is an important part of stockpiling resilience so that the next headwind doesn't bring the organization to a stop or blow it off course. When an organization has courage, it can more effectively identify and address its blockers. It can also be more effective in understanding and accepting the situation.

The *reinventing resilience* model's core—collective self-efficacy and staunch realism—is like the unique life-giving brackish water of an estuary. They combine to give an organization the courage to face its blockers and the situation. But the estuary is only generative when the freshwater and seawater flow continuously. Organizations can renew resilience by building internal capacity to identify and address blockers as well as understand and accept the situation.

IDENTIFY AND ADDRESS BLOCKERS
What holds an entire organization back? What are the enigmatic forces that create or stop organizational momentum? *Blockers* are forces that stop, slow, or misdirect an organization. Each organization has its unique combination of blockers that, when activated, can kick-off a collective fight, flee, or freeze response.

Blockers lie beneath the surface and pop up when activated. Think of a friend who's afraid of dogs. They tense up when they see a dog coming at them. The dog is a blocker that creates a fear response. If your friend examines many encounters they have had with dogs, they may discover that they had a scary confrontation with a dog earlier in life, so their fear response is now the default.

This can happen at scale in organizations. With courage, organizations can identify and address the blockers that lie beneath the surface. Here are some ways to do that:

KNOW YOUR HISTORY
Doing an organizational timeline exercise to identify not only the major successes but the shared failures and disappointments helps put things in perspective. Making note of the real blockers that rippled through an organization can be surprising. They can include major world events (like an economic slow-down) or deeply personal shared moments (like a beloved colleague dying). Knowing the history of the organization helps not only identify blockers but puts them in context.

RECOGNIZE PATTERNS
Asking questions about your organization's history can provide rich experiential data to mine. For example, when did the company feel most alive? Most like a family? Most transactional? Most siloed? Is there a connection between these responses and the events from your organizational history? Recognizing patterns helps leaders understand default responses to challenges and gives them space to decide if a different response would be more effective.

HAVE A DELIBERATE DECISION-MAKING PROCESS
Author April Rinne in her book, *Flux: 8 Superpowers for Thriving in Constant Change*, suggests that we "run slower."

Slowing down is one of the most effective ways to address blockers. Impulsive responses come from the primal brain and are instantaneous. More rational responses come from the thinking brain but take a bit more time. Deliberate organizations give themselves an extra beat and some additional space to think collectively and *choose* how to respond to a blocker—rather than responding impulsively. Having a decision-making process that includes time for reflection and thought forces the collective brain of an organization to slow down a bit and creates opportunities for folks to call out familiar patterns of behavior that may not serve the organization.

ADMIT WHEN THE ORGANIZATION IS STUCK
Leaders and their teams are not perfect, so there will be times when blockers are not identified. It is important for leaders to admit the moment they feel like a collective response to a situation is fear-based. Getting stuck in this way happens a lot in toxic or unhealthy organizations. Workers spend loads of time talking and worrying about the leader's potential reaction to something instead of working. Calling out the collective "freeze" mode can help the group refocus on what it can control (e.g., work quality) and let go of what it can't (the capricious boss reaction).

CALL TIME-OUT
Toyota famously had the Andon cord that enabled any worker on the assembly line to pull a cord to stop production... for any reason. It took courage to give that much autonomy and control to front-line workers. Workers felt trusted with that

level of responsibility, and they did not abuse or misuse it. Leaders that create conditions for all workers to pause the process help build courage in their organization.

I saw the leader of a logistics company call an impromptu meeting in the middle of their vast call center. He stood on a makeshift stage and reflected on the current quarter's results and his role in creating a culture that, essentially, was slowing the company down. He apologized and invited others to reflect. For about forty-five minutes, the company stopped and talked about the reality of the situation. People felt energized and, most importantly, led.

UNDERSTAND AND ACCEPT THE SITUATION

It takes courage to understand and accept the situation for what it really is versus what you may want to be. It's surprisingly difficult to get an accurate picture of the situation. When we do, we might reject what we discover because it is painful to see.

Getting an accurate picture is difficult because, as humans, we tend to create the reality we want to see. We use biases, assumptions, and cognitive short-cuts to stitch together what ends up being our perception, memory, and ultimately our reality. Doing the work to get as clear a picture as possible takes courage.

It also takes courage to accept the situation once you see it for what it is. For individuals in therapy, the practice of *radical acceptance* involves exploring and determining those things that are within and outside of one's control.

Some of the hallmark qualities of radical acceptance, according to Tara Brach, clinical psychologist and author of *Radical Acceptance* are:

- The understanding and belief that whatever discomfort we are currently feeling, it's temporary.

- The ability to reconcile our desire for control with the fact that some events are random.

- The avoidance of common thinking traps like:

Generalizing—which is drawing a conclusion by making an inference

Catastrophizing—which is over-indexing on the negative aspects of a situation

- Avoiding certain language patterns like using "always" and "never" to describe our situations.

For organizations, there are several ways they can understand and accept the challenging situation that they are facing:

PART WITH POLLYANNA

Pollyanna thinking—or irrepressible optimism—is a form of reality avoidance that can cause costly delays and erode morale... not to mention undermining one's credibility as a leader. There's nothing wrong with optimism, but too much of it can be disastrous in organizations. It's fine and healthy to contextualize reality with examples of what's going well, but avoiding the difficult truths skews reality and makes resilience harder to build.

ACKNOWLEDGE THAT IT MIGHT BE PAINFUL

Accepting the situation sounds easy, but when the situation is dire or very difficult, people tend to want to avoid it. Trying to truly understand the situation involves challenging one's interpretation or challenging others' interpretations. That's not easy, and when jobs and results are on the line, it can be tense and painful.

When leaders prepare themselves and the rest of the organization for a journey of discomfort, they are committing a courageous act of leadership. Steve Wright, Stacey McDaniel, Dinesh Patel (whose story follows), and Scott Hill (who you will read about later) have been excellent in acknowledging how difficult and even painful the road ahead might be.

FIND COMFORT IN THE SHARED JOURNEY

If you want to go fast, go alone. If you want to go far, go together. There is comfort in the ancient African maxim. Difficult journeys are made easier when you have others by your side. Subsuming oneself into the group, elevating the whole, and distributing authority and power takes courage. It also builds trust and resilience for the inevitable challenges ahead.

I once consulted to an executive team in the fashion industry. They were among the best I've seen at unifying. They hashed out their differences in the board room, but once the group decided on a direction, they operated with one voice. Nobody outside that group would ever see even a smidgen of dissent. They collectively owned the shared journey.

BREATHE LIKE A SEAL

US Navy SEALs are trained not to panic in the water because they know that panic leads to death. Box breathing, or 4-4-4 breathing, is a way SEALs focus on what they can control to gain perspective over a challenging situation they're facing. Breathe in for a four-count, hold for a count of four, and exhale for a four-count. This technique—done literally or figuratively as a group—is helpful in the civilian world in moments of uncertainty or volatility (e.g., workplace accident, sudden stock price drop, or hostile takeover) because it buys time for the thinking brain to come back online.

FIND BEAUTY IN THE TRUTH

Think of the classic movie *The Matrix*. The main character moved between versions of reality and, eventually, as Neo began to see patterns and understand it all, he found beauty and curiosity in it... even when it was basically a postapocalyptic hellscape. Steve from Jay Peak (Chapter 4) did the same thing when he called dozens of brides-to-be who were worried the resort would force cancelations of their wedding plans. He found beauty in that hard truth and showed it to the engaged couples. Organizations that punch through their self-limiting beliefs are capable of profound innovation. It's not easy to get there, but looking for beauty even in the unappealing truth can help you accept the situation for what it is and move forward with confidence.

COURAGE IN ACTION: PROTAGONIST THERAPEUTICS' MOMENT OF TRUTH

On [Friday] March 23, 2018, our stock price was $20.43. On Monday, when we announced the news, the market didn't spare us. We were beaten up, so on March 26, we were at $8.75, and a month later, $5.50.

Dinesh Patel, CEO of Protagonist Therapeutics

Protagonist Therapeutics, founded in 2006, has built a platform that makes it safe to orally administer immunomodulating drugs that treat chronic diseases like Inflammatory Bowel Disease (IBD) and others. Patients with chronic conditions will typically take a drug for the remainder of their lives to manage the disease; and many of those drugs are administered via injection.

A safe, orally-administered alternative is a game-changer for folks—like me—whose knees get weak even thinking about needles. Moreover, orally administered drugs treating gastrointestinal diseases can stay "gut-centric," as Protagonist CEO Dinesh Patel states, rather than having an injected drug "spinning in your bloodstream from head to toe."

Protagonist's innovation in discovering and developing novel peptide-based drugs through its proprietary platform has enabled it to secure several global research partnerships. It also has attracted attention from investors seeking shareholder returns. Innovation and success created an upward spiral of visibility, investment, and expectations.

In the mid-2010s, Protagonist was developing an IBD drug called PTG 100, and clinical trials were promising... so promising that the drug was the cornerstone for their IPO. In the world of drug development, trials are disciplined and regulated procedures. Lots of steps, lots of data. The science must play itself out. But it's also common to share interim data so folks (like investors) can understand a prospective product's market potential.

Two hundred forty patients were in the multiyear PTG 100 trial. Because of its design, researchers could conduct an interim analysis after about eighty patients completed treatment. After that analysis, a *futility decision* is made. That means an independent committee reviews the data to determine whether the study should continue or if it's *futile* to keep going. Part of the futility decision involves comparing patients treated with PTG 100 with those treated with a placebo.

Dinesh was encouraged by the data he and his scientists were seeing, so he began meeting with investors to let them know the futility study would happen. This gave investors an opportunity to jump in with some assurance that the trial—while not complete—was heading in the right direction.

Then, March 23, 2018, happened. It was a Friday. Dinesh and his team were waiting for the results of the futility study and fully expected to be "popping champagne" when they got the independent validation of the study's efficacy. At 2:30 Pacific time, Protagonist's medical director came into Dinesh's office. "The outcome was futile," he said simply.

"Now, this guy did have a sense of humor," Dinesh said. "So, for a few seconds, we were like, 'Oh, he's just pulling our leg.'"

"And he's like, 'No, I'm serious. The outcome is futile.' And we were just shocked and in total disbelief."

They chilled the champagne, but this blast of bad news called for harder stuff. "We had to settle for bourbon," Dinesh said.

The science brains in the room quickly hypothesized that a placebo error must have caused the determination. Trials need to have some—but not too many—people on a placebo to compare the drug's effects to other similar patients. Having too many patients in the placebo group introduces statistical noise, which makes it harder to single out the drug's effects in treating the disease.

This hypothesis proved true. There were too many placebo patients. The futility determination had been made not because of the drug, but because of human error in conducting the trial.

Dinesh and his team didn't learn the full truth about the botched trial for several days. But the market was expecting news about the futility decision that Friday. Dinesh shared the negative outcome in a press release. Predictably, the company's stock tanked.

All that work. All that time. All that money. Gone because of an unforced error.

Let's look at Protagonist Therapeutics' inflection point through the lens of the *reinventing resilience* model. While Dinesh's upbringing in India, combined with his business success, gave him self-belief, that wasn't sufficient for the organization to grow through this big challenging period.

The collective efficacy of Protagonist's teams enabled the organization to not only absorb the bad news but quickly move forward with a new plan for the drug. With an acknowledgment of reality, they were able to get to work learning from mistakes, shoring up areas for improvement, and rectifying the situation.

COURAGE TO ADDRESS BLOCKERS AND UNDERSTAND THE SITUATION

Staunch realism and collective efficacy powered Protagonist's courage to face the situation for what it really was: terrible. But they also were able to manage their collective emotional reaction to prevent a fight, flee, freeze response. Other leaders might go on a blame-finding expedition or "read people the riot act." But fear-inducing tactics only activate survival mode and block higher-order problem-solving when it's most needed.

After Dinesh and the team at Protagonist Therapeutics discovered a human error in their medical trial, something remarkable happened.

Dinesh looked at the situation for what it really was. He didn't tell marketing to *spin* it into a positive narrative, and he didn't look for heads to roll. His staunch realism approach enabled him to bypass the blame game and focus on the future and new possibilities.

"As scientists, we live in a world with high failure rates," Dinesh said. "So we dug our way through."

Protagonist Therapeutics lives in a world of possibility, seeking new solutions to complex medical problems. It understands and acknowledges its past but doesn't live there. Dinesh is confident that with time and additional successes, the narrative on the street will shift.

But Dinesh is not forcing it.

"We may be in the penalty box for a long time," he said. "But we may be able to make something out of this and prosper even better than we imagined before. So it's the longer route and maybe a nonscenic route. But eventually, it leads to our destination and beyond." Dinesh Patel's resilience—cultivated over decades—scaled to the organizational level, and, as a result, the company grew through a significant challenge.

The relationship between the CEO and the rest of the organization is often fateful. I remember in my executive coaching certification program at Case Western Reserve University, Dr. Richard Boyatzis talked about the impact of leaders' behavior on companies. "To you, it may be a whisper," he said as if speaking to a CEO. "But to them, it's a scream." We instinctively look to leaders, pick up signals from them, and over-index on reacting to them. "Emotions are contagious," Dr. Boyatzis often said. And the CEO is the super-spreader when it comes to emotional contagion.

Oddly, it's difficult to recognize our courage, even when there's a lot of evidence that we have it. I couldn't find it when I was stuck in the Grand Canyon. We must always be reminded that we can face the situation and our internal blockers. Being in an environment that reinforces collective efficacy and staunch realism has the effect of powering courage.

A COURAGE PARABLE: CARROTS, EGGS, AND COFFEE

A young woman went to her mother and told her about her life and how things were so hard for her. She did not know how she would make it and wanted to give up. She was tired of fighting and struggling. It seemed as one problem found a solution, a new one arose.

Her mother took her to the kitchen. She filled three pots with water and placed each on the stove. Soon the pots came to a boil. In the first, she placed carrots. In the second, she placed eggs. In the last, she placed ground coffee beans. She let them sit and boil without saying a word.

In about twenty minutes, she turned off the burners. She fished the carrots out and placed them in a bowl. She pulled the eggs out and placed them in a bowl. Then she ladled the coffee out and placed it in a bowl.

Turning to her daughter, she asked, "Tell me, what do you see?"

"Carrots, eggs, and coffee," the daughter replied.

Her mother brought her closer and asked her to feel the carrots. She did and noted that they were soft. The mother then asked the daughter to take an egg and break it. After pulling off the shell, she observed the hard-boiled egg. Finally, the mother asked the daughter to sip the coffee. The daughter smiled as she smelled its rich aroma. The daughter then asked, "What does it mean, mother?"

Her mother explained that each of these objects had faced the same adversity—boiling water. Each reacted differently.

The carrot went in strong, hard, and unrelenting. However, after being subjected to the boiling water, it softened and became weak. The egg had been fragile. Its thin outer shell had protected its liquid interior, but after sitting through the boiling water, its inside became hardened. The ground coffee beans were unique, however. After they were in the boiling water, they had changed the water.

"Which are you?" she asked her daughter. "When adversity knocks on your door, how do you respond? Are you a carrot, an egg, or a coffee bean?" (UT Austin, 2021)

COURAGE AT SCALE

The boiling water we will likely remember forever was the continuous change brought about by the COVID-19 pandemic. It threatened our livelihoods and, for many, it was a peak moment of stress. The stress we felt was that of death. That was the staunch reality of the situation.

It took courage to face this situation collectively. It truly sucked, and it felt overwhelming for most of us. Humans don't like threats, and as we've already learned, we've developed some deeply ingrained responses to them. The responses we've developed are designed to make the threat go away. We are hard-wired to resist threats. That's what makes it hard to see a situation for what it is.

Sometimes it's easier to downplay or avoid a situation: to conclude, "it's not my problem." Other times, it feels better to make the situation so huge it can't possibly be solved or so tiny that it's not worth paying attention to. These are ways we help our brain avoid big threats. But resilience means having a way to bypass all those forms of resistance.

Of course, a lot of times, it feels better to fight reality. If you're old enough to remember John McEnroe's famous outburst at Wimbledon, he screamed at the chair umpire after a linesman called a ball *out*. "YOU CAN NOT BE SERIOUS!" McEnroe yelled. "CHALK FLEW UP!" He was fighting reality and authority because he didn't want to accept that the ball was actually out. For McEnroe, accepting reality was harder than causing a scene, arguing with the chair umpire, and nearly getting thrown out of Wimbledon.

Do you have the courage to identify and address blockers? to accept and understand the situation? I opened this chapter comparing the reinventing resilience model to a hummingbird. Hummingbirds have boldness and bravery that outsize their tiny bodies. They are nimble, can fly in any direction, can hover, and are incredibly quick. These qualities fuel and justify their courage. Courage is possible for our organizations and us when we understand the qualities that fuel our courage.

CHAPTER SUMMARY
- Courage is the ability to face and deal with something even when we are afraid of it.

- Building organizational courage helps stockpile resilience, so the next headwind does not bring the organization to a stop or knock it off course.

- Courage enables organizations to identify and address blockers—the forces that slow, stop, or misdirect an organization.

- Courage also enables organizations to understand and accept the situation.

- The situation can be difficult to see clearly from an organizational perspective. Practicing radical acceptance at scale builds courage.

* * *

Scan the QR code below for more information and resources specific to this chapter.

CHAPTER 7
Confidence

We are twice armed if we fight with faith.

PLATO

FAKE IT UNTIL YOU MAKE IT?

The *reinventing resilience* model's core—collective efficacy and staunch realism—is like the brackish water in an estuary. Saltwater and freshwater combine to create a thriving ecosystem. Courage, discussed in the previous chapter, is a source of resilience in the model. The other is confidence. Confidence enables organizations to access all their resources and discover realistic possibilities to move forward at speed and scale.

When I was a kid in the 1980s, I vividly remember an antiperspirant commercial with the tagline, "never let them see you sweat." If you did sweat, you not only looked bad but also you were seen as a hair's breadth from losing control. Naturally, the solution was to drown the affected area in a chemical that kept your sweat, smell, and—implicitly—your emotions inside. The underlying message was you could fake it until you made it. Just cover up your fear, and—poof—you're confident.

Swagger, PR stunts, fancy buildings, and signing bonuses are all outward signs of organizational self-assurance. And it's important for organizations to be intentional about others' perception of them in the world. But that's different from the confidence necessary to build resilience. Let's explore.

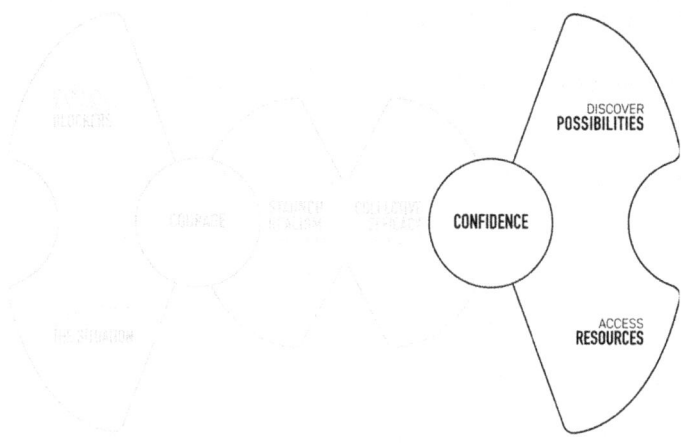

Resilient organizations have confidence to access resources and new possibilities.

WHAT IS CONFIDENCE?

Organizational confidence exists not within workers but rather in the space between them. Relationships, culture, and ways of working rely on the implicit rules of an organization. Those rules are built on the countless interactions between workers every day. When guided by values, principles, or a clear strategy, we get greater cohesion and trust between the people and—as a result—stronger organizational confidence. Confident organizations have a vibe of certainty about and firm trust in their workers—even though outcomes are not guaranteed.

Patagonia's values provide the source for high levels of confidence and trust within the company. Besides fleece vests and backpacks, Patagonia is also well known for its quirky and magnetic corporate culture. The company fearlessly expresses its corporate values in a variety of ways. For example, one core value is "Not bound by convention," so not only does the company provide free onsite childcare at its Ventura, California headquarters, it pays for nursing moms to bring their babies and a nanny along on business trips. They also live by "Use business to protect nature," which has driven their advocacy to preserve indigenous lands and encourages customers to repair (not replace) products to keep them out of landfills.

Authenticity has created a trusting workplace. Ninety-one percent of employees believe Patagonia is a great place to work, according to their website, and 84 percent of employees would recommend the company to a friend, according to Glassdoor.

HOW TO BUILD ORGANIZATIONAL CONFIDENCE

Building organizational confidence enables organizations to take the hard steps needed for transformational change. Change is like walking into a valley. It's unclear what will happen down there, so without confidence, it can feel too scary even to take the first step. When people feel triggered into fight, flight, or freeze mode, they fall into survival mode—the rational mind is cut-off, and all we've learned and all that's possible become harder to access. Our primal brain is in control.

Organizations can build collective confidence much the same way their workers can. In the introduction, I talked about my terrifying moment in the Grand Canyon. I got scared, and I lost my confidence. But my guide helped bring my rational brain back online. He reminded me that I was capable and experienced. He also showed me a new and different possibility—that of success. When an organization can access its resources and imagine new possibilities during a time of peak challenge, it's because it has the collective confidence to do so.

ACCESS RESOURCES

In my decades of consulting, I have seen many organizations encounter significant challenges. Many of them react as if it's the first difficult moment the organization has ever faced. It is uncanny. A collective panic attack sets in, and the organization gets stuck in a gap-closing mindset. The pressure to alleviate the pain is a reflexive response. "Make it stop," bosses cry!

When this happens, the immediacy of the challenge makes it harder for workers to access examples of similar challenges they faced in the past. Or they fail to take time to access workers' capabilities. Or they circle the wagons instead of reaching out to trusted advisors or stakeholders who can provide calm, objective counsel.

This collective amygdala hijack happens a lot in organizations. However, with collective confidence, organizations can tap into *resources* to build resilience. Here are some ways to do that:

WHAT GOT YOU HERE MIGHT GET YOU THERE

If you have ever been lost in the woods, you might remember the moment when you started to look at everything differently. Pine needles became a bed. The sun became a compass. Water became as precious as gold. Circumstances can force us to look creatively at commonplace things—people, infrastructure, processes, wins, clever but abandoned ideas—to gain perspective and reduce the feeling of collective overwhelm.

Every organization has hallmark qualities of its culture. Don't overlook them. Those qualities are very useful in building resilience. For example, pragmatic or objective organizational cultures could be very good at staunch realism. Hopeful and optimistic cultures could have a wellspring of collective self-efficacy.

TAP INTO SKILLS AND KNOWLEDGE

Every worker has a story. Every team has an achievement. Every product, initiative, business development win, or campaign has tapped into the skills and knowledge of the organization. For whatever challenges an organization faces, it also has amassed technical skills, experience, expertise, and adjacent skills they can apply to it.

Diverse, cross-functional, or skip-level teams often outperform homogenous teams because they are open to exploring the inert potential of the team members. This can scale to the organizational level, but it must be done intentionally to build collective confidence. The YMCA, responding to the food shortage during the pandemic, tapped into its strong local networks and knowledge of local resources, like unused county vans, to adapt and expand services.

LOOK BACKWARD TO MOVE FORWARD
History can be a great teacher. A global workwear company I worked with was struggling with low employee engagement. The company was more than fifty years old, and the brand had become a household name; it was in growth mode. But workers believed the company was *old school* and disinterested in workers as people. When we paused to catalog the organization's track record of innovation and employee acknowledgment, mindsets started shifting. As a result, the company created cool collaborations with digital influencers to extend the brand to new audiences. Highlighting historical moments of achievement can reduce the psychological barriers to organizational success.

INVOLVE MULTIPLE PERSPECTIVES
There are two strategies to employ if you happen to be attacked by a bear on the trail. You must play dead if it's a Grizzly and fight back and try to escape if it is a Black Bear. The strategies are not interchangeable, so picking the wrong one could prove fatal. That's where bringing multiple perspectives into the mix comes in. Relying on your own flawed or foggy recollection is far riskier than working with others.

Stakeholders who are outside the day-to-day can often provide a clarifying perspective. But their wisdom is often neglected in the interest of time or pride. Stakeholders is a broad term that can include industry connections, community partners, vendors, suppliers, and shareholders.

WORK WITH WHAT YOU'VE GOT
Sometimes it's better to use what you have than spend time creating new resources. I worked with a global communications company that was struggling to unify its messages across its many advertising campaigns. Every product or region, it seemed, had its own strategy; this led to products competing with each other in key markets.

The long-term solution was to create an integrated dashboard to house and display all marketing and advertising activities and make them available globally. But that solution would take months to develop and roll out. We used what we had in the interim: spreadsheets! It was a cumbersome, unattractive manual process. But it worked as a temporary solution and provided visibility into activities across the enterprise.

DISCOVER POSSIBILITIES
In the Canyon, I didn't initially think I could take another step without falling off the cliff. Then, with Adam's help, I saw that I could make it to the end of the section… and out of the canyon… and back home to my family. The same happens at scale in organizations. It is challenging for organizations to see the full range of possibilities when they get stuck.

They sometimes hire consultants to facilitate a discussion that's meant to shine new light on a situation and craft an action plan for results. However, sometimes well-intentioned consultants begin brainstorming possibilities without considering the organization's blockers, situation, or resources. This can lead to a colossal waste of time as flip charts fill with far-flung, pie-in-the-sky ideas that will never, ever happen.

Possibilities are not fantasies. There's nothing wrong with dreaming. Letting the mind run wild is valuable, but constraints are known to direct creativity toward more constructive ends. The *reinventing resilience* model offers a framework to ground possibilities in reality.

To identify your organization's possibilities, consider the ideas below:

USE GOOD FILTERS

Imagining possibilities can feel like standing at the fork in the trail. It can feel daunting and fateful. But ultimately, you must choose a direction. Good filters can help you narrow your options and feel more confident about the direction you're heading. Filters can include your personal or organizational values, strong data, consensus from the group, or whatever information you trust that will enable the organization to proceed together.

LOOK AS FAR AS YOU'RE COMFORTABLE

If you've ever stood at the top of a mountain, you may have been struck by how small and insignificant you feel. Staring across the ranges can feel overwhelming; you just got to the top of this mountain, and now look... more mountains! In organizations, leaders need to be careful to point the organization toward a target that's both challenging and inspiring. Too easy, and nobody gets motivated. Too hard, and workers get burnt out. Look as far as necessary to activate your organization's collective confidence.

KNOW AND SHARE ORGANIZATIONAL GOALS
In the October 1947 issue of the popular periodical *Collier's Weekly*, cartoonist George Lichty depicted a uniformed airplane pilot casually addressing his passengers saying, "We're still lost, but we're making good time."

Organizations can confuse incremental successes with progress. I've heard the same complaints from line workers and first-level managers for more than twenty years consulting in organizations of all sizes. Many do not know where the organization is going. Leaders often feel like they're being transparent, but workers often need a frequent consistent message before it truly sinks in.

BREAK DOWN ROUTES INTO SEGMENTS
Setting ambitious goals is a good thing. And it can be tremendously inspiring to be part of a bold plan if it's framed in the organizational reality, seems possible, and won't burn workers out to get there. Conquering Everest, for example, is a bold goal. Getting there, however, requires a lot of equally inspiring interim steps. Possibilities may need sub-possibilities to keep the momentum and confidence level high.

AMPLIFY THE ENCOURAGING VOICE
In organizations, there are a lot of competing voices. But who is worth listening to? Is it the die-hard optimist, the yes-person, the nay-sayer, the pragmatist, the philosopher? Well, think of who you would want behind you when you're climbing up a steep trail. The voice of encouragement is probably what keeps you motivated and confident that you can make it up the hill. While it's important to give everyone

a chance to speak, the encouraging voices powered by confidence will be the ones helping identify possibilities. It's worth amplifying them for the benefit of the whole.

CONFIDENCE IN ACTION: ALL AMERICAN ENTERTAINMENT

The events industry was at the epicenter of "adapt or die" during the turbulent and uncertain years of the pandemic. Adapting to a volatile environment requires clear thinking, and All American Entertainment was a role model for poise under pressure.

All American Entertainment represents clients seeking high-quality professional speakers for events around the world. Their business is delivering a message in the form of a person that aligns with their client's specific needs. For example, suppose a company is having a big annual meeting. In that case, it might call AAE to book a keynote speaker whose story syncs up with the meeting's overarching themes and strategic imperatives.

If you've never been behind the scenes at a big corporate event, it's something to behold. Companies carefully curate and orchestrate their events. They painstakingly craft end-to-end experiences that seek to create a specific vibe, mindset, or sentiment for the guests. Guest speakers—like Sir Richard Branson, Martha Stewart, Serena Williams, and others represented by AAE—are invited to generate enthusiasm, reinforce key messages, and add credibility.

But in the spring of 2020, everything stopped. As the reality of COVID-19 set in, conferences, meetings, and other entertainment events were canceled. Margo Dunnigan, COO of All American Entertainment, told me ten million dollars worth of events disappeared in just a couple of weeks. At that time, according to Dunnigan, people were in shock and "not embracing virtual" as an option. Thinking back to that time, "you get a little PTSD," she said. "In the month of May [2020], we did as much business as we typically do in a couple of days," Dunnigan said.

While revenue dried up and clients struggled to figure out what to do, AAE acted. It furloughed some folks, cut salaries, enacted a work-from-home policy, and stayed tuned-in to their clients while they game-planned their next steps.

Dunnigan never let her clients see the company sweat. But their poise came from organizational confidence, not a "fake it until you make it" strategy. In an all-hands-on-deck effort, the company retooled itself to meet the increasing demand for virtual events. What ordinarily would take months, they accomplished in days or weeks. They created an entirely new pricing model and engagement contracts for speakers. This gave clients access to nearly the full portfolio of speakers, and speakers were relieved to have a renewed supply of events.

The AAE team worked with the brave, trailblazing clients who moved their in-person events to virtual. They created an internal Slack channel to crowdsource information about how to run virtual events successfully. They had an all-hands meeting to discuss this new reality. They equipped the sales team to discuss virtual options with clients. And they trained up an ad-hoc team as the internal virtual event experts to be a resource to sales and the rest of the company.

"It was rocky at the start," Dunnigan says. Not only was the team coming up to speed, but they also discovered that virtual events with headline speakers (like the kind they find for clients) drew much bigger audiences than anticipated. Of course, communication providers like Zoom and Microsoft Teams were experiencing huge surges in usage, so sites were lagging and crashing, disrupting events.

As challenging as it was to watch from AAE's perspective, client feedback was positive. Most indicated that they would do virtual events again. Bookings started increasing, and by the end of the year, all furloughed workers had come back, those who took salary cuts were made whole for lost income, and the company even added headcount.

Reflecting on the experience, Dunnigan talked about the depth of change at AAE because of the disruption. Not only did sales and marketing undergo changes to their routines, but talent contracts also had to be reworked (they now have separate virtual pricing for speakers). In fact, they surveyed more than thirty thousand speakers to set virtual speakers fees. It was a massive undertaking.

The pandemic was a difficult and valuable learning experience for AAE. The company's staunch realism and collective efficacy powered their confidence to tap into resources and imagine previously unimagined possibilities. In the months that followed the most challenging days, AAE integrated what they learned, adapted their practices to a new way of delivering value, and imagined a wider set of possibilities on an accelerated timeline. AAE is positioned for stronger growth today than it was before the pandemic (and prepandemic growth looked good). As Dunnigan says, "We see the future bigger now. We see ourselves achieving our longer-term goals sooner as a result of this."

CONFIDENCE IN COMMAND: THE USS BENFOLD

Not many leaders can imagine positive possibilities when faced with a seriously messy challenge. When they are, most leaders prefer to start from scratch. Change takes too much time, they believe, so it feels more efficient to take an "out with the old, in with the new" approach.

However, a scorched earth approach has a lot of unintended consequences. It feels good to the leader because change is *happening*. But everyone else ends up operating out of fear. The work of "change" then becomes an act of compliance, and very little loyalty or trust is built along the way. The culture gets built on a shaky foundation weakened by cynicism and blind compliance.

When Mike Abrashoff first stepped onto the USS Benfold, many considered it the worst ship in the Navy. Under his leadership, one of the US Navy's most modern warships became a model of performance. In a remarkable turnaround, the Benfold was singled out as having the best combat readiness in the Pacific fleet, the highest gunnery score, and the lowest rate of key equipment failures. The ship's crew completed training missions in record time, and 100 percent of its career sailors signed on for an additional tour of duty, compared to 54 percent for the rest of the Navy. Morale for the rest of the crew also became excellent.

Abrashoff got these great results by focusing on his crew. "When you shift your organizing principle from obedience to performance, the highest boss is no longer the guy with the most stripes—it's the sailor who does the work... My job was to listen," Abrashoff said. "To see the ship from the eyes of the crew." He started asking every crew member what they liked about their ship and what they wanted to change. He then identified nonvalue-added tasks that caused the most dissatisfaction and proceeded to tackle them.

Stainless steel bolts replaced some of the ship's parts and a specially coated metal that did not require constant painting. The youngest sailors, who dreaded the constant chipping and painting, were delighted. He arranged for college-bound sailors to take the SAT in Bahrain, and he formed a partnership with an internet provider to allow sailors to stay in touch with their families. He rejected naval food provisions, switched to purchasing lower-cost brand names, and used the savings to send his ship's cooks to culinary school.

Abrashoff knew every one of his three hundred crew members by name. He wanted to help them "chart a course through life. ... I consider my job to improve my little three hundred-person piece of society." Interestingly, although the Benfold and its commander did not focus on strict discipline, there was no lack of respect or cohesion on the ship. The crew willingly saluted its commanding officer, and there was a strong sense of duty and cooperation.

Abrashoff states: "I have to prepare higher-level people to step into leadership roles. If all you do is give orders, then all you'll get are order takers. Removing many of the nonreadiness aspects of the job—from chipping paint to cleaning—lets us spend more time on learning". Abrashoff's caring for his crew, his ability to listen to them, his relative disregard for rules while focusing on performance, and his focus on improving quality of life have created enviable results.

Captain Abrashoff realized he got a terrible assignment and could have gone through the ship focused only on all the attitudes and infractions he needed to fix. Of course, he saw them. Instead, he focused his attention in a different direction. He focused on possibilities. Instead of asking, "How do I bring the ship into compliance?" he asked. "How might this ship become the best in the Navy?" The question was fateful, and it took a lot of confidence to believe in untapped resources even he couldn't see. As a result, he liberated the inert potential of hundreds of sailors and created a great organization aboard the Benfold.

CONFIDENCE IN HISTORY: SHACKLETON AND THE CREW OF THE ENDURANCE

Ernest Shackleton and his ship Endurance set sail in August 1914 for Antarctica with a bold, potentially history-making goal. He and his team would be the first to walk across the continent, starting from the coast of the Weddell Sea, crossing the South Pole, and ending up at the Ross Sea.

In January 1915, the vessel came within sight of the Antarctic mainland. But harsh winds and cold temperatures descended quickly, and the sea ice trapped the ship.

The Endurance was immobilized and held hostage to the drifting ice floes. Shackleton realized that his men would have to wait out the coming winter in the ship's cramped quarters until summer's thaw.

Shackleton feared the potential effects of his men staying on board with not much to do more than he did the ice and cold. He required that each man maintain his ordinary duties as closely as possible. Sailors swabbed decks; scientists collected specimens from the ice; others were assigned to hunt for seals and penguins when fresh meat, a protection against scurvy, ran low.

He also kept a strict routine for meals and insisted that the men socialize after dinner as a tonic for declining morale. Still, collective disappointment rose, and tempers flared.

Through the routines, order, and interaction, Shackleton sought to manage the collective fear that threatened to take hold when the trip didn't go as planned. He knew that in this environment, his greatest enemies were high levels of anxiety and disengagement, as well as a slow-burning pessimism.

Days became weeks, and weeks became months, and still, the ice held the ship. By June 1915—the thick of winter in the Southern Hemisphere—the ship's timbers were weakening under the pressure created by the ice, and in October, water started pouring into the Endurance.

Shackleton ordered the crew to abandon the sinking ship and make camp on a nearby ice floe. The next morning, he announced a new goal: "Ship and stores have gone—so now we'll go home."

In the privacy of his diary, he was more candid about the gauntlet in front of him. "A man must shape himself to a new mark directly as the old one goes to ground," he wrote. "I pray to God I can manage to get the whole party to civilization."

After the Endurance sank, leaving the men stranded on the ice with three small lifeboats, several tents, and supplies, Shackleton realized that he himself had to embody the new survival mission—not only in what he said and did but also in his physical bearing and the energy he exuded.

He knew that each day, his presence had a huge impact on the men's mindsets. He managed his own emotional intelligence—to use a modern term—to keep his own courage and confidence high; when these faltered, he never let his men know.

Just as important, Shackleton kept his men's focus on the future. The ship was gone; previous plans were irrelevant. Now his goal was to bring the team home safely, and he improvised, adapted, and used every resource at hand to achieve it.

When a few men expressed skepticism about his plans, he acted quickly to contain their opposition and negativity by trying to win them over and keeping close watch on them. He assigned several potential troublemakers to his own tent on the ice, proving the value of the saying, "Keep your friends close and your enemies closer."

By April 1916, the ice began breaking up, and Shackleton ordered the men to the lifeboats, hoping to reach land along the tip of the Antarctic Peninsula. After a week of stormy seas, they arrived at the deserted Elephant Island. They were exhausted, seasick, and dehydrated. But they took "childish joy," one scientist wrote in his diary, "in looking at the black rocks and picking up the stones, for we had stepped on no land since Dec. 5, 1914."

Almost immediately, Shackleton began planning his next move. Along with five other men, he managed to guide a twenty-two-foot lifeboat to South George Island; from there, a smaller party reached a whaling station and got help. After a meal, a bath, and a change of clothes, Shackleton said, "We had ceased to be savages and had become civilized men again."

Then he began looking for a vessel capable of rescuing the rest of his crew. During the next several months, he set sail in three different ships, but none could cut through the ice surrounding Elephant Island. Finally, on August 30, 1916, aboard the Yelcho, a Chilean steamer, Shackleton sailed within sight of the island and rescued the twenty-two remaining men. "I have done it," he wrote his wife, Emily. "Not a life lost, and we have been through hell."

Shackleton leaned into staunch realism and collective efficacy. He acknowledged the situation for what it was—dire—but did not change the leadership structure of the crew. He was in charge; there was no consensus decision-making. At the same time, he believed that the ship's structured, hierarchical culture was its ticket home. He helped the crew maintain the narrative that they could and would eventually get home, even if it took a while.

As a result, the crew tapped into not only their personal and physical resources but also the possibility of survival. And their options were guided by a clear-headed view of the situation—even when they shifted their strategy. They stayed with the ice-bound ship. That made sense at the time, but after it broke apart, they needed to start walking. Then on South George Island, he only took a few crewmembers onward to seek civilization—putting faith in the remaining crew that they would be alive when he returned for them.

CONFIDENCE CAN SCALE
When confidence is high, organizations can take bold steps to accelerate transformation. Leaders play the role of guiding their organizations into a valley of the unknown, so trust is critical. They help organizations access resources and imagine new possibilities during times of peak challenge.

For example, Shackleton's journey was before modern antiperspirants, but he never let his crew see him sweat. He built team confidence, and that made all the difference in elevating resilience to the point every single man survived a perilous expedition. Leaders like Dinesh Patel led a company through an unexpected challenge and kept it from dwelling on the past. And Margo Dunnigan and her team at AAE accessed the range of resources at the company to pivot on a dime.

CHAPTER SUMMARY
- Confidence is an organizational quality that exists in the white space between workers.

- Building organizational confidence creates greater cohesion and trust between workers, which, in turn, creates a stronger organization.

- Confidence helps organizations identify and access resources and discover possibilities.

- Resources include the qualities of the organization, the amassed skills and knowledge, and external supports like professional networks, community connections, and other stakeholders.

- Possibilities result from and help build resilience when they are realistic, practical, and grounded in the organization's reality.

* * *

Scan the QR code below for more information and resources specific to this chapter.

CHAPTER 8
Life in the Estuary

*If you do not change direction, you may
end up where you are heading.*

LAO TZU

In Chapter 5, I likened the *reinventing resilience* model to an estuary. I framed it as a life-giving place that thrives because of its unique position at the intersection of freshwater and seawater. Its brackish water supports a richly diverse and abundant ecosystem. In that respect, the estuary serves as a perfect metaphor for the source of organizational resilience.

But estuaries are complex, and they cease to thrive when their delicate ecological balance is upset. External forces can act on them, or they can die from within when either the freshwater or saltwater stops circulating. So, estuaries need a continuous flow of both fresh and seawater or they collapse.

The same is true for resilience in organizations. When staunch realism and collective efficacy are flowing, and in balance, the organization feeds its courage and confidence to grow through challenges. In this chapter, we will survey several organizational types through the lens of the *reinventing resilience* model and conclude which types are likely to thrive and which ones are heading toward extinction.

REJECTING RESILIENCE'S PARADOX

Imagine sitting at a table and you see before you a sponge and a steel rod. You are asked to pick them up one at a time and feel them. You pick up the sponge. It's the kind for washing cars. It's big, soft, orange-yellow. It's dry and super light. You give it a good squeeze, and when you release your grip, it returns to its original shape.

Now, you pick up the steel rod. It's cold, firm, and has a black-rusty color. It looks like a piece of rebar. It's heavier than it looks. Naturally, you grab it with both hands and try to bend it. It resists. Your hands turn white where you exert pressure, but the bar is pushing back. It retains its shape despite your attempts.

Which one is resilient? The sponge is resilient because it bounced back from the *adversity* of being squeezed. The steel rod, on the other hand, is resilient because it resisted the pressure applied to it and held fast.

In truth, both are resilient. But they lack the kind of resilience that would enable them to grow through their challenge. They simply survive their challenge. They don't thrive. Their resilience is lifeless, automatic, and almost transactional.

Reinvented resilience—the kind that organizations need—is a living resilience that feeds organizations and helps them go beyond the point of setback to the point of growth and thriving.

ORGANIZATIONS ARE HUMAN SYSTEMS

From the first tribes to the first settlements to today's global companies, humans have been hardwired to function in groups. But, as much as humans have an affinity for groups, we seem to have a love/hate relationship with them. As time goes on, we grow dissatisfied with our group structures and change them. We tend to leave behind models of working together when they no longer served us.

Perhaps our organizational structures grow and fade the same way estuaries collapse. When there's a disruption in the flow of collective efficacy or staunch realism, organizations can lose courage and confidence, become brittle, and eventually break. As society changes, our preferences for ways of working change. Old models struggle, and new ones take their place.

Today, workers are increasingly rejecting older, less resilient organizations that stubbornly adhere to their underlying structural assumptions. They want new, more resilient organizations that offer a source of purpose, passion, equity, and inclusion. Where some have seen a great resignation, it may be the beginning of a great migration:

From	To
Old, Less Resilient Organizations	**New, More Resilient Organizations**
Hierarchical	Pluralistic
Process-focused	Purpose-driven
One right way	Values-based
Drink the Kool-Aid	Empowerment
Quarterly goals	Democratization
Innovation through optimization	Everyone's a leader, decider, innovator
Silos	Shared decision-making
Accountability and Incentives	Equity
	Stakeholders
Meritocracy (climbing the ladder)	Comfort with complexity
Growth	Voice
Shareholders	
Speed	

A RESILIENCE TOUR

Humans have reinvented their organizational structures over time, but they are not lost to history. Many types still exist today and can be found in businesses, nonprofits, and government agencies. I use the term "organizations" very broadly in this book, but we are focusing on more formal types where people come together to do work.

For this tour, we will explore the *reinventing resilience* model in the context of some familiar organizational types. I borrowed Frederic Laloux's framework when looking for types of organizations to apply the reinventing resilience model to. His book, *Reinventing Organizations*, does a nice job framing organizational structures as well as the underlying feeling many had working in them. I felt this best captured the "life" of the various organization types.

THE POWER-CENTRIC ORGANIZATION

Power-centric organizations do not really care about workers. There is generally one very strong leader, and everyone else has the leader's permission to be there. The leader directs all the activities, and nobody makes a move without his or her approval. Like a wolf pack, everyone is constantly sizing each other up, and any sign of weakness is met with a direct challenge. It is valuable to be the leader in power-centric organizations since workers are subject to his or her authority. Street gangs or mafias are examples of power-centric organizational systems.

The closest I got to working in this kind of organization was back when I was doing education reform work. I was part of a nonprofit organization that ostensibly provided services to schools in a low-income, historically underserved urban area. However, my organization was one puzzle piece in a larger scheme to advance a political point of view and, ultimately, change school funding laws.

For it all to work, the strategy and funding of my organization, the schools, and other supporting organizations were controlled and orchestrated centrally. And the central organization was impatient with workers who questioned their motivations or brought ideas that distracted from their narrow political objective. It was a tribe, and it became clear that allegiance was the most highly valued attribute. After a short period of expansion, the network folded in on itself... unable to deliver on the political promise.

I participated in this knowing what was going on. But I believed, in the end, helping provide a high-quality education to kids who otherwise would be relegated to low-performing local public schools was noble. I focused on that and did my best to avoid the nasty political end of the stick. They say politics is like watching the making of sausage. When I became president of one of the organizations in "the network," I saw the process up close. I was not a good fit. I wanted to call out the sausage-making, but I knew that was career suicide. I struggled with being hamstrung by the *higher-ups*, offered strategies they hated, and eventually presided over the organization's (mutually agreed) phase-out.

Turning to the *reinventing resilience* model, this organization scored high on collective efficacy: the bosses believed they could weather any storm. But they lacked staunch realism. In these kinds of tribes, the leader believes he (usually male) can hold onto power because he has a *better plan,* uses more force, or generates more riches for members. It often ends with a violent transfer of power from one leader to the next. Because neither the organizations nor their members can break out of that cycle, resilience dissipates.

THE LOYALTY-CENTRIC ORGANIZATION

Loyalty-centric organizations center around conformity and self-discipline. There are complex rules in these types of organizations, and following them is expected and rewarded. Leaders value allegiance, duty, formality, and conformity, as well as adherence to the hierarchical organizational structure. Organized religions, armies, and some universities are examples of loyalty-centric organizational systems.

These organizations fail the "courage to face the situation and blockers" part of the *reinventing resilience* model. These organizations are like steel rods, very rigid and resistant to any bending pressure. They may be resilient in the classic sense of *strong* or *persistent*, but their fidelity to rules, structure, and tradition make change very, very slow. So slow that they often reflexively double-down on their outmoded structure when they realize they've failed to keep up with the times. Only when there's an enormous amount of pressure do they either break or adapt. Think of what it took for these seemingly sensible changes to happen: the US Army accepting LGBTQ+ service members; South Africa rejecting decades of apartheid; or Soviet states separating themselves from "Mother Russia."

I worked at an organization like this once. A venture capitalist had recently purchased the company from the founder, and I came in as part of a new strategy to provide consulting services to an impressive network of customers. The owner, not surprisingly, wanted to see his investment pay off. He brought in a CEO to "turn the organization around." The CEO, in turn, brought in a group of trusted advisors and friends to help "with the transition."

We had a brand, and the CEO thought we could capitalize on that. The swag started flowing. Bottles, backpacks, stickers, fleece vests, you name it. The expectation was that we were to *represent* the brand while emblazoned with the uniform. Loyalty, compliance, and conformity meant you could keep your job. Stepping outside the lines meant you got an invitation to *a meeting* where they asked you to turn on your friends or leave. They fired me from that place. Thank God.

THE EFFICIENCY-CENTRIC ORGANIZATION

Efficiency-centric organizations value smart, nimble decision-making. These organizations are like machines built for speed, so structures to support discovery and innovation are common. Rigidity and rules keep the efficiency-centric organization humming along to achieve its endless growth potential. Most of today's publicly traded companies, global corporations, and start-ups are efficiency-centric organizations.

Efficiency-centric organizations can survive their way through one major challenge after the next. But thriving is not a priority. These organizations often have mottos suggesting empowerment or fresh thinking. But, ironically, many of these organizations fail to have confidence in their people. They fail to access the full potential of their human resources.

I consulted for a large energy company during a watershed moment in its history. An environmental disaster created regional damage on a historic scale, and the company's culture was ultimately to blame. Its mechanistic mindset created a culture whereby a checklist managed everything. Everything had a procedure associated with it. I once visited the global headquarters, and there was a sign with instructions on how to use the stairs.

The overemphasis on process squeezed out every ounce of humanity. The treatment of workers was like cogs in a machine. And they learned their voices were not welcome. They were generally terrified to call out warning signs to their supervisors for fear of repercussions. Errors, missteps, sloppiness accumulated and BOOM—a catastrophe. People were the solution, but the company provided no space or safety for workers to speak up. Silence, complicity, and compliance were valued higher in that culture than speaking truth to power.

THE FAIRNESS-CENTRIC ORGANIZATION

Fairness-centric organizations are less structured and more pluralistic systems. They have a flatter organizational hierarchy, and they enable ideas and inputs to flow from any corner of the organization. The prevailing sentiment is that everyone has value to the organization, so workers are expected to speak up to provide input regardless of their roles.

These organizations have several qualities that make them more likely to be resilient when seen through the lens of the *reinventing resilience* model. For instance, because they invite, welcome, and include a variety of perspectives in their planning and decision-making, they tend to have a keen understanding of the situation. Their inclusive nature creates higher levels of trust, making them more likely to access resources.

On the flip side, fairness-centric organizations can meander toward consensus-driven decision-making. If they over-index on consensus, it could end up becoming a blocker that prevents or slows work efficiency. Additionally, because every voice is heard and counted equally, fairness-centric organizations could spend more time than most creating and sorting long lists of possibilities... even impractical ones.

I was a graduate assistant when I was studying for my first master's, and my duties included attending meetings related to the student activities at the university. Every idea and decision had to have thoughtful consideration in a group comprised of students, faculty, and university staff. In one case, we discussed booking on-campus entertainment for the following semester. There were about eight to ten slots for entertainers spread out over the thirteen-week semester.

However, the group generated at least seventy possible acts. Then we had to narrow the list down. It took ages. Everyone felt heard, but we also were exhausted by the process.

THE HUMAN-CENTRIC ORGANIZATION
Human-centric organizations, according to Laloux, rest on three pillars: self-management, holism, and evolving purpose. They have strong internal ways of working that encourage, enable, and trust people to make the right decisions (without running every decision up the flagpole). There is structure, and people have roles, but these organizations operate as a holistic system where workers are interconnected and interdependent. And human-centric organizations pay attention

to purpose and make it a practice to revisit and evolve it as the context in which it operates changes.

From the *reinventing resilience* model perspective, human-centric organizations have many strengths. Their commitment to evolving purpose is a sign of their staunch realism. They choose to look at the world without filters, understand and accept that the world changes, and are prepared to evolve their purpose to thrive through the next wave of change.

Human-centric organizations are self-reflective but don't navel-gaze. Their courage gives them the ability to identify past patterns of behavior, withhold judgment about past decisions, acknowledge blockers that got in their way, and move on from those moments.

I'm fortunate to work for a human-centric organization. Daggerwing Group, a global top ten change management consultancy, operates with a pluralistic mindset. There's structure *and* shared responsibility and decision-making. The values are ever-present and woven into every interaction. I've never worked in a company so attuned and committed to the professional development of everyone at all levels. The work quality is exceptional because everyone feels both responsible and able to participate. As a result, Daggerwing can attract amazing people and clients to keep it all going strong.

But is it a resilient organization according to my model? First, Daggerwing Group is not a commune. It's a business. Over time, however, it has evolved through very challenging circumstances to become a strong, disciplined, purpose-driven organization. The leadership team has a very clear understanding of the competitive business environment within which it operates (Staunch Realism) and an unshakable belief that it can do a better job at change management than any consulting company (Collective Efficacy).

The result is a lot of courage and confidence. And they've put it in writing. Daggerwing's beliefs are doing right by people, the power of audacity, and owning our future together. The beliefs are more than just words; they are visible in recruiting, business development, resourcing, recognition, individual development, benefits, and much more. Daggerwing thrives during the daily challenges that it faces. It is a resilient organization that continues to stockpile resilience for unforeseen challenges.

OF LIFE CYCLES AND ESTUARIES

Blue crabs in the Chesapeake Bay rely on the great estuary for survival. Each stage of crabs' life cycle occurs either in the fresh water near the river inlets, in the muddy brackish water of the estuary, or in the salty ocean water. The estuary is the life-giving ecological system through which the crabs pass back and forth several times during their lives.

Organizations also have life-giving forces they rely on to grow through their difficult times. The *reinventing resilience* model's core: staunch realism and collective efficacy comprise the brackish water that enables organizations to thrive through the challenges they face daily.

CHAPTER SUMMARY
- When staunch realism and collective efficacy are flowing, and in balance, the organization feeds its courage and confidence to grow through challenges.

- Resilience is both strength (steel rod) and flexibility (sponge). But organizational resilience is a living resilience that feeds organizations and helps them go beyond the point of setback to the point of growth and thriving.

- Organizational structures have changed over time. Some older, less effective structures remain. But human-centric organizational structures are emerging to accommodate workers' needs.

- Human-centric organizations tend to be more attuned to the needs and desires of current and prospective workers and therefore enjoy an advantage. The pandemic exposed the need for workers to be seen as people at work and not cogs in a machine.

* * *

Scan the QR code below for more information and resources specific to this chapter.

CHAPTER 9
Dwelling in Possibility

I dwell in Possibility
A fairer House than Prose
More numerous of Windows
Superior – for Doors
Of Chambers as the Cedars
Impregnable of eye
And for an everlasting Roof
The Gambrels of the Sky
Of Visitors – the fairest
For Occupation – This
The spreading wide my narrow Hands
To gather Paradise

EMILY DICKINSON

CHANGE BRINGS POSSIBILITY

If change is so scary, why do we do it all the time? Scientists have long said the only constant is change. Yet humans always seem so surprised when it happens. We're incredulous when our favorite coffee shop closes. We lose our minds when road construction forces a detour. If you watch social media, you'll see people expressing their emotional reactions to bad weather, the change of seasons, days getting shorter (or longer)—all of which happen every year. #notsurprising #cantcontrolanyofthat

On the other hand, maybe we're hypocrites. We sign up for change all the time. We get married, we get and change jobs, we move out of our parents' house, we have kids, we even meet new people. These are all things we do to ourselves. We invite change into our lives and celebrate it when it happens to others. I mean, the event planning and party sector of the US economy is around $4 billion, according to Statista. There were five million one hundred thousand home sales in 2021 in the United States, and nearly three hundred fifty thousand babies are born every day in the world (The World Counts 2022). Change is part of our lives, and we invite it.

When we talk about resilience, we often only think of it in terms of a big, surprising, negative change. It comes out of the blue and either knocks us down, sets us back, or gets in our way. However, we rarely talk about resilience in the context of bringing positive possibilities.

THE STORY OF MY NAME

In 2016, I traveled with my wife and son to Austria and Slovakia for vacation. I had been a teacher in Bratislava years earlier and kept in touch with the amazing family that basically adopted me while I was there. We flew into Vienna and, since it was around Christmastime, we planned on touring the city for a couple of days before heading east to Slovakia.

After our long flight, we dragged our luggage to the Kaiserhof hotel near the center of Vienna. The staff greeted us, and during the check-in process, the desk clerk collected our passports as is the procedure. But he stopped and fell silent when he opened my passport.

"Thallner, eh?" He said. "You know that's an Austrian name?" Of course, I did. My dad was born near Salzburg, and despite living for forty years in Birmingham, Alabama, he never stopped sounding like Arnold Schwarzenegger.

"Yes, I know. My dad's from here." I said.

"Do you know what this name means?" he asked.

"Well, I'm not sure. I think it means valley, right?" I guessed.

"Well, not exactly," he said. "*Tal* means valley, but your name is T-H-A-L," he spelled it out as if I needed the help.

"Actually, it's an old-time occupation," he said. "Back in the old days, people would need to travel from one valley to the next valley. Sometimes they would take their cows, or they had family on the other side of the mountains. They would hire a 'Thallner' as a guide to help find and safely cross the mountain pass."

VALLEY TO VALLEY
Kodak's well-documented downfall illustrates what happens when companies stay in their valleys, fail to access their "thallners," and operate with an outdated definition of resilience.

Steve Sasson was an engineer at Kodak when he invented the world's first digital camera. That was in 1975. Today, we slap our foreheads in disbelief. How could Kodak be so far ahead of the pack on this technology only to file for bankruptcy just thirty-seven years later?

Kodak's valley was film. Their brand was synonymous with quality film. Even legendary singer/songwriter Paul Simon wrote a hit song about their top film product, "Kodachrome." Kodak's strategic orientation was film, and their fundamental strategic error was believing pictures had to be printed. It could not think beyond it. They bought oPhoto in 2001 to encourage consumers to print more photos. They continued meandering in their own valley while their competitors packed their backpacks, hired thallners, and made their way to the next valley.

Kodak, like so many other companies, believed it was taking strategic action. And it was. But it failed to acknowledge the reality that there were other valleys to explore. And climbing over the mountains would have enabled them to learn, adapt, and see differently. Instead, they looked at the steep hills on either side of the valley and just walked straight down the path of least resistance.

Back when record players were a thing, music lovers took great care to protect the vinyl discs. We carefully held the record by the edges thinking our finger oils would rub the music off or our nails would scratch the surface. Once placed on the turntable, we'd put our faces right down at record level to ensure the needle fell ever so slowly and exactly in the right spot. Getting it in the groove meant we could hear the song we wanted.

This is how I think about Kodak and so many other companies that have failed to embrace positive change. Companies get content in their groove. They would rather stay in their own lane and perform the tune they already know well.

There are countless examples of companies that failed to look up from the valley floor and see opportunity in the mountain passes. Blockbuster, for example, was a leading VHS rental chain whose business model relied on consumers owning (and knowing how to use) videotape machines. Moreover, they failed to welcome change, and users found a more convenient solution—Netflix would send CDs to your house.

MySpace, Sears, Yahoo, PanAm Airlines. These major companies were in their own valleys, and although they each ruled their sectors at one point, they ultimately decided to wander parallel to the mountains instead of climbing them. Their end-to-end journey in their one valley was like a needle stuck in the record's skipping rut. Their lack of staunch realism caused them to lose sight of the horizon.

BLISS IN THE ABYSS

But some companies welcome change and adapt to it. They recognize what they can and can't control and quickly respond to market shifts. They do what they can; they gamble; and they often win.

For these resilient companies, they move laterally across the landscape. Mountains are not barriers, but they're part of the path. So are valleys—deep and unfamiliar, they are often fertile. Resilient companies learn while they're in the depths of their valleys *so that* they can get out of them.

They believe there's bliss in the abyss, so they're not afraid. They recognize the importance of valleys to strengthen them for the journey through the challenging passes. For example, Netflix spent time in a few valleys. They first were a distributor of CDs. Originally, you had to pick your movies, and they would send them in order of how you picked them. You couldn't get the next one until you returned the previous CD. Then, it became a digital streaming service which they still are today. But they are also a major content creator that's outperforming old, established producers.

As Ricky Gervais said when he hosted the 2020 Golden Globe Awards,

No one cares about movies anymore. No one goes to the cinema. No one really watches network TV. Everyone is watching Netflix. This show should just be me coming out, going, "Well done, Netflix. You win everything. Good night."

Similarly, Minnesota-based Ecolab started in 1923 as an industrial carpet cleaner manufacturer called Economics Laboratory. The founder initially saw an opportunity to clean wall-to-wall carpets when he saw a stain on the carpet in a hotel room. Over the decades, the company crossed many valleys and climbed many peaks. They added petrochemical processing, metalworking, transportation, and laundering to their portfolio.

But their expansion and commitment to water safety and sanitation was a significant move. After decades in the chemical business, they are all-in on providing clean water to communities across the globe. Their company attracted the attention of Bill Gates, who went on to become EcoLab's largest shareholder.

Organizations that look at valleys and see a long, steady path confine themselves to a static reality. But those that see the valley as a fertile learning ground and refueling stop accept a bigger reality. They find bliss in the abyss and move on.

RESILIENCE IN CONFLICT: CALIFORNIA'S STANDARDS WAR

Speaking of valleys. Let's talk about California—home to the great Central Valley. It's also where you would go to find some of the most challenging education policy fistfights in the nation. In the early 2000s, Governor Pete Wilson appointed me to serve as a staff member to the California Academic Standards Commission. Our remit: determine what every child should know and be able to do as a result of their K–12 education. That is, write the blueprint from which all curricula would be built.

Pundits and policy-makers expected us to fail. Other states had dabbled in creating statewide academic standards. Their processes were expensive, drawn-out, special interest feeding frenzies that mostly ended up lowering the bar for students and schools. However, there were powerful incentives (by that, I mean money) from the Federal Elementary and Secondary Education Act that caused California to get the ball rolling. Everyone knew it would provide a point of coalescence for every political ax-grinder in the state. The legislature formed a commission, partisans drew battle lines, and the governor's office hired a staff.

Our small, nonpartisan team was an ensemble cast of smart, dedicated, irreverent mavericks with impeccable ethics. It was the first time any of us had worked together, but we had instant chemistry. We believed in each other, and we believed in what we were doing. Our leader, Scott Hill, kept us relentlessly focused on creating sound policy for the students of the state.

"Think about the work we did on science standards and how easily that could have failed," Hill shared with me recently. "We had two bids [from subject matter experts (SMEs) representing opposing political/education ideologies], and we faced impossibly irreconcilable choices. We faced enormous political pressures from the Republican governor's team and from the Democrat-led California Department of Education. How could we possibly achieve the state's goals as well as fulfill the mission assigned to the commission if we picked one SME over the other?"

We were standing in the valley, faced with a choice of picking someone. Choosing either SME would have created political fallout, nullified our nonpartisan approach, damaged our credibility, and escalated an already tense ideological fight. Instead of limiting ourselves to the choices available in the valley, we looked for a better view on higher ground.

"I recall a number of conversations among ourselves and our attorney, and we ultimately decided that there was only one clear path forward," Hill said. We had to work with both, and they had to work together. We rejected both bids and negotiated with both parties to get them at the same table, working side by side in the best interest of kids, not just their own self-interest.

"We knew that we were bringing inside the tent, so to speak, all of the public agitation and fighting we expected over science but believed we could find ways to manage the conflict," Hill said. "We also knew we'd face some public scorn and skepticism for rejecting the bids because we could not expose our strategy." We had to take our lumps, of course. Publicly, the SMEs and their legions bashed us for rejecting them. Privately, however, they were more than happy to have a seat at the table.

Possibilities are an important part of the reinventing resilience model. Bold, new possibilities—like bringing in warring parties to work together on statewide education policy—emerge when the *reinventing resilience* model is functioning well. The team was brimming with collective efficacy. As Scott Hill says, "[we had] an absolute belief that we'd reach the finish line and complete the job." We also had incredible contextual acuity that gave us the courage we needed to play in the big leagues. When we needed it, we had a stockpile of confidence to help us access surprising possibilities.

RESILIENCE AND TIME: SLOVAKIA'S TRANSFORMATION

I grew up frightened by Russia and fascinated by its reluctant neighbors that comprised the Union of Soviet and Socialist Republics (USSR). TV programs tried to make me believe that it was a soulless place full of dead-eyed drunks, clever spies, and paranoid ushanka-wearing leaders with nothing better to do than watch parades and pick fights. But I also knew many people wanted to leave and couldn't. There were people there, and I wanted to meet them.

I finally could go to central Europe and see it for myself. With the help of Kamil Vajnorský and his amazing family, I was fortunate enough to teach English in a high school during the first year of Slovakia's independence. I'll never forget the sense of *possibility* everywhere I went. I worked on campus at the *Ekonomická Univerzita v Bratislave* full of entrepreneurial students who *knew* they had a chance to make a huge impact on the country's economy and position in the world.

Back in 1968, it was very different. Alexander Dubček was elected First Secretary of the Communist Party of Czechoslovakia and began decentralizing authority and loosening restrictions on media, speech, and travel. Feeling threatened, the USSR and other Warsaw Pact countries invaded Czechoslovakia to repress the reforms in what became known as the Prague Spring.

"Nobody would help us," Kamil's daughter Ľubica said to me about that time in her country's history. One of the only ways citizens could express themselves during the period of Soviet rule was through sports. "Now you know why we get so excited when we play Russia in hockey," she said with a smile.

When I got to Bratislava in the 90s, it was a new country having amicably separated from the Czech Republic. Slovakia was freshly independent and filled with hope and possibility. Quickly dropping the Soviet façade, the country could freely celebrate its unique and rich Slovak heritage. It was gorgeous to see and such a privilege to be there. Today, Slovakia is part of the European Union and the North Atlantic Treaty Organization. Its borders, once heavily guarded, are open. People come and go; businesses flourish and flounder; it all feels so... normal.

Sometimes spending time in the valley isn't a choice. Slovakia had to walk through a long, dark valley for decades before emerging as a strong country with a vibrant economy. It didn't waste its time while it was down there. The country leveraged its collective courage to see the situation for what it was. It also leveraged its collective confidence to access resources, like high-quality education and cultural identity, and imagine bold, new possibilities. When its time came, it was ready.

THROWING OPEN THE WINDOWS OF POSSIBILITY

During a family vacation to Austria, we took a cable car to the top of the Untersburg, an alpine massif not too far from Salzburg. It was December, and we were heading into an alpine climate, so we put on all our winter gear. It was what skiers call a "blue bird" day: absolutely crystal-clear skies and fresh snow. And while the temperature was only twenty degrees Fahrenheit, the intense sun warmed us. We could take our jackets off, walk the trails comfortably, and enjoy the magnificent view.

We had no idea it would be that amazing. We would never have experienced it if my wife hadn't insisted that we go. She encouraged us to try something new, and it was not only worth it, it was life changing.

We change all the time. We welcome it. When we dwell in possibility doors and windows open to new futures we couldn't imagine. We can't get to the next peak to see the next horizon unless we trudge through the valleys. But there's learning down there, and what we take with us enables us to appreciate and persist through the cold, windy mountain passes to enjoy the sunny peaks.

CHAPTER SUMMARY

- We invite change into our lives, and even that change requires resilience.

- Valleys are narrow and limiting, but also places to learn and grow.

- Traveling laterally across the landscape (over hill and valley) is harder and more rewarding than traveling along a valley

- Organizations can learn in their valleys so that they can get out of them.

- Resilient organizations—and countries—leverage time in valleys to imagine new possibilities.

- There's bliss in the abyss.

* * *

Scan the QR code below for more information and resources specific to this chapter.

Conclusion

I felt frozen in the desert. Fear had rendered me unable to take another step. I opened this book with my Grand Canyon story to illustrate how suddenly someone could find themselves overwhelmed with fear. I also shared it because, on the surface, it was about my perseverance or grit. It was also a story about Adam, my guide, who helped me through the incredibly difficult process of becoming "untriggered" enough to move forward.

From Adam's perspective, he saw someone who had already hiked thirty or forty miles over several days in desert conditions below the rim of the Grand Canyon. He understood that I was physically fit but mentally distracted because we had spoken several times around the campfire about my brother-in-law's death.

Moreover, Adam had hiked these trails many times before. He was a seasoned hiking guide and was equipped with experience and expertise. He had an ample supply of courage and confidence, which kept him from being triggered in the same way I was. That enabled him to use his excess capacity to help me.

He was like a tidal force restoring balance to the estuary. He allowed me to tap into his self-efficacy and staunch realism so that I could build some courage and confidence to not just get unstuck, but to proceed along the trail. I didn't know it at the time, but that moment was the beginning of the *reinventing resilience* model.

In this book, my goal has been to be your organization's Adam—a *thallner*. I have aimed to help you see that your organization—whether it's a small business, a global corporation, a nonprofit, a cross-sector collaboration, a community, or even a country—can get stuck just like a single worker can. We can use some lessons from the resilience research to help find a way forward at scale.

COLLECTIVE EFFICACY + STAUNCH REALISM

Witnessing the Russian invasion of Ukraine reinforced my belief that resilience is all about growing through challenge. The collective Ukrainian response is a perfect example of how resilience scales and a perfect way to summarize the model.

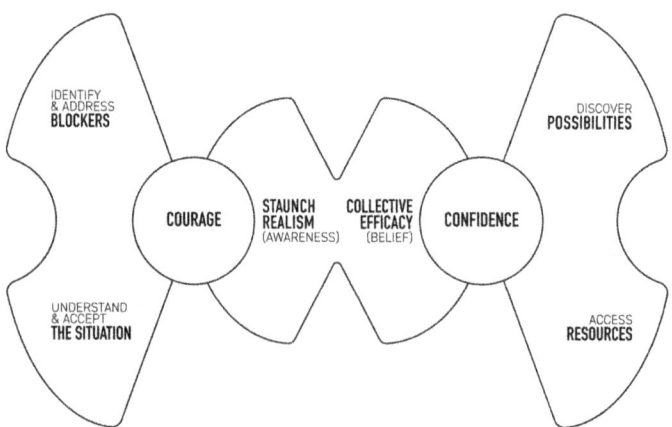

Consider the reinventing resilience model in the context as large as a country

Collective efficacy and staunch realism are two mutually supporting qualities that act like the brackish water of an estuary. The mix of freshwater and seawater flowing in and out creates a unique ecosystem, but you must have both for it to work. There is a collective belief among Ukrainians that they can and will defend their sovereign nation. I heard a CNN reporter interviewing a woman who stayed behind to make meals for the soldiers. "Why don't you leave?" the reporter asked. "I'm not the one who should leave," she snapped. "The Russians should be leaving."

But there's a very clear awareness of the gravity of the situation. For weeks before the invasion, reports and pictures were circulating of civilians receiving weapons training. They knew the situation was gravely serious and, despite not wanting to believe Russia would "actually go through with it," they acknowledged the reality that it could happen.

COURAGE AND CONFIDENCE
The outputs of collective efficacy and staunch realism are courage and confidence. Courage and confidence are the life-giving qualities that propel us through the strong headwinds blowing in our faces. They also provide us with clarity and resolve to point ourselves in a direction we *need* to go while leaving behind the direction we might *want* to go.

Courage enables us to identify and address things that trigger our fight, flee, or freeze responses. It also enables us to understand the situation more fully and completely.

Confidence allows us to identify possibilities that may have seemed out of reach or unworthy of mention. It also allows us to tap into resources that we often forget about when we're in panic mode.

For the Ukrainian people, their courage and confidence help them focus on the ominous task of repulsing a Russian invasion while so much emotional anguish is flooding their collective mind: families torn apart, refugees, explaining the situation to kids, leaving behind the elderly or disabled, knowing that no other country's troops will come on their soil to fight with them.

IT'S TIME TO REINVENT RESILIENCE

Imagine if Adam from the Grand Canyon worked in a toxic workplace. What if his boss was passive-aggressive, played favorites, or didn't have Adam's back? If Adam was checked-out because his job was "such a drag," then what would he have done when I got stuck? Would he have acted with compassion, calmness, and confidence? Would I be alive to write about it?

Organizations today have bought-in to a narrative that "solving problems" is what they exist to do. Of course, organizations must solve problems. However, they exist to do a lot more than that. We hold ourselves and our organizations back when we hang onto the deficit-based definition of resilience. We end up in a perpetual gap-closing cycle—endlessly responding to "setbacks" while grinding workers down and limiting our organization's growth potential.

We need to reinvent resilience as a capability that scales across the enterprise. It's more than building the resilience of each worker. We must focus on the organization as its own entity: getting the whole to build ITS collective efficacy and ITS staunch realism more comprehensively. Because, when it does, powerful positive narratives will flow through the organization and help teams and departments find the courage and confidence to grow through challenges, not just survive them.

WHAT TO DO NOW

BE ADAM

You've gotten this far. In your career. In your life. In this book. You have likely seen organizations focus so hard on the gap-closing cycles that they are susceptible to a heavy impact when the next "big challenge" comes along. Maybe you work in one. Maybe you have a client like this. Maybe you run an organization, community, or country that could be described this way.

Be their Adam. Be their *thallner*. You can be the guide that helps your organization look up from the valley floor to see new possibilities just over the mountains.

Use the *reinventing resilience* model to help your organization grow through challenges. Jump start their collective efficacy and staunch realism. Sit with them while they struggle to get "unstuck" the way Adam did with me, and the way I try to for the companies I serve. Help them: understand what's keeping them stuck, access resources, see the reality of the situation, and identify new, practical possibilities.

REINVENT RESILIENCE

This book is like a long thought experiment. It's not a doctoral thesis. I didn't conduct original quantitative research. I curated a lot of thinking from a lot of people and pushed it through the food mill that is my mind. My hope is that my curiosity and attempt at organizing some thinking around this topic will encourage you to rethink your own organizations.

I hope you think of your organization as a set of possibilities rather than a set of problems to be solved. I hope you use your ability to reframe things from problems to possibilities—like the British Airways example in Chapter 1. And I hope you shake off the notion that resilience is all about bouncing back. That is just not sufficient. We can no longer afford organizations that put workers in gap-closing roles. Neither must organizations exist solely to close gaps. It's time for a fresh look at how organizations can thrive in our ever-changing world.

THINK BIGGER

One of the challenges of researching this book was finding examples of resilience at scale. I had to wade through a lot of information about resilience, which made me realize that we've been self-limiting in our perception of resilience. To be honest, very few people are thinking about how resilience can be applied to organizations let alone countries.

Of course, if you're not feeling particularly strong, and you're not able to be a "thallner" for your organization, please don't. Take care of yourself first. If you have the capacity—like Adam did, for example—to help a group, team, or organization, then please do. Frame the conversation as an opportunity to build resilience for the next inevitable challenge. While stark, it's honest. And it signals that it's time to speak out loud what everyone's already thinking: more change is coming.

* * *

Scan the QR code below for more information and resources specific to the conclusion.

Acknowledgments

I extend thanks to all the people who helped with this book.

Special thanks to my interviewees for sharing challenging organizational experiences and their perspectives on resilience: Steve Wright, Stacey McDaniel, Jeffrey Snyder, Stephanie McElhone, Sokthea Phay, Jason Lippert, Amber Selking, Dinesh Patel, Jami Taylor, Margo Dunnigan, and Jennifer Best.

My perspective was built on the wisdom of so many extraordinary colleagues, teachers, and mentors I've had over the years, and I'm truly grateful for their generosity of spirit. To my friends, colleagues, and spirit animals at Case Western Reserve University's Weatherhead School of Management, The Garthwait Leadership Center at Gettysburg College, The Teal Team, Take Back Work, and Daggerwing Group, I am truly grateful for your support. To my past coworkers who shaped and influenced my thinking, I thank you.

I'm truly grateful for the generous support of these sponsors that made this book possible:

- Roque Versace and his team members at Troops

- Scott Hill and his colleagues at The College Board

- Andrew Hughes and staff of the Garthwait Leadership Center at Gettysburg College

- Chris Gassman at the Center for Sustainable Business at the University of Pittsburgh School of Business.

Reinventing Resilience was also fueled by the backing of an enthusiastic group of supporters who placed a bet on me and this effort. They got on board early and formed a supportive community that read early drafts of the book, helped me select the final book cover, and provided loads of encouragement. I can't thank enough these amazing folks who contributed to the book campaign and rooted me on throughout my writing journey: Irene Bassock, Elizabeth Bollo Leatherbee, Ann Bomberger and Justin Gingerich; Monica Brewster, Davina Brown, Amy Buchanan, Vania Bueno Cury, Keith Chamberlain, Randi Edgar, James Feen, Linda Figueiredo, Candie Fisher, Maximo Gamez, Brian Gittens, William Gretzula, Andrea Griffith, Lauren Grimshaw, Erin Hazen, Melissa Hersh, Christine Hoover, Sharyn Horowitz, Judy Issokson, Gerald Jannicelli, Brandi Jauregui, Michele Johnson, Anne Lackritz, Debbie Levine, Jack Li, Andrew Liang, Maureen Maier, Travis Marsh, Brian McClinton, David Meeker, Susie Miller Carello, Laurie Minott, Hilary Naiberk, Makenzie Newman, Meg Parker, Patricia Petty, Kate Philips-Kaiser, Ian Phillips, Diana Rivenburgh, Valerie Rivera, Olivia Rowan, Chris Rudolph, Anil Saxena, Jerry Scala, Nikole Schmidt, Luisa Schumacher, Laura Slover, Matthew Spaur, Elizabeth

Stocker, Van and Nancy Stringham, Barry and Edie Tepper, Elaine and Jeff Thallner, Karl and Marian Thallner, Pete and Amy Thallner, Anton Thallner, Konrad Thallner, Katarina Thallner, Brynn and Colin Thallner-Pomerantz, Christopher Thornton, Whit Tice, Kristen von Donop, Tom Wagner, Glen "Surfboard" Walker, Allyson Webster, Jim Young, and Karen Zeccinelli.

Several people had a particularly profound and specific impact on the book, and I'm lucky and grateful to call them family, colleagues, and friends. I extend a special thank you to:

- Anita Brodie—my mom—whose experience sparked my quest to eliminate workplace stress

- Tanya James who's early thought partnership and willingness to have Zoom calls 12 time zones apart led to the initial version of the resilience model

- Ed Frauenheim whose optimism, creativity, encouragement, mentorship, and coaching got this project off the ground and moving forward and whose heavy pen truly made this book better.

- Gregg Vanourek provided compassionate and thorough feedback, regular encouragement, and a great hike in the Colorado hills.

I'm particularly grateful to research assistants Fadekemi Agboola and Jessica Allesi, who were creative, professional, and delightful to work with. Also, I dearly appreciate Ian Allison and Antonio Dorileo for bringing my reinventing resilience model to life with a simple, powerful image. I thank Kathy Wood, Rachel Mensch, Erik Koester, and the New Degree Press team for their abundant resources, cheerful assistance, and unbridled encouragement. Mariya Bentz thoughtfully built the *Reinventing Resilience* website.

Finally, my wife Pam and son Max were always by my side during this writing journey. Their support was so much more than giving me time and space to write. They hiked the peaks and valleys with me. Every fist bump, every early morning coffee, every reminder that it's getting late, every time Max and I were writing at the same time… I felt supported, loved, and encouraged. I couldn't be more grateful to them.

Paul

Appendix

INTRODUCTION

CCH Incorporated. "Costly Problem of Unscheduled Absenteeism Continues to Perplex Employers." CCH press release, October 12, 2005. http://hr.cch.com/press/releases/absenteeism/default.asp.

Druss, B. G., Rosenheck, R. A., and Sledge, W. H. "Health and Disability Costs of Depressive Illness in a Major US Corporation." *American Journal of Psychiatry* 157 no. 8 (2000): 1274–1278. https://pubmed.ncbi.nlm.nih.gov/10910790.

Hoel, H., Sparks, K., and Cooper, C. *The Cost of Violence/Stress at Work and the Benefits of a Violence/Stress-free Working Environment.* International Labour Organisation, 2001.

Johnston, K., Westerfield, W., Momin, S., Phillippi, R., and Naidoo, A. (2009). "The Direct and Indirect Costs of Employee Depression, Anxiety, and Emotional Disorders: An Employer Case Study." *Journal of Occupational Environmental Medicine* 51 no. 5 (2009): 564–577.

McGregor, Jena. "This Professor Says the Workplace is the Fifth-Leading Cause of Death in the US" *Washington Post.* March 22, 2018. https://www.washingtonpost.com/news/on-leadership/wp/2018/03/22/this-professor-says-the-workplace-is-the-fifth-leading-cause-of-death-in-the-u-s.

National Institute for Occupational Safety and Health (NIOSH). Stress At Work Booklet. Publication No. 99–101.

Perkins, A. "Saving Money by Reducing Stress." *Harvard Business Review* 72 no. 6 (1994): 12.

Pfeffer, Jeffrey. *Dying for a Paycheck: How Modern Management Harms Employee Health and Company Performance—And What We Can Do About It.* Harper Business: 2018.

CHAPTER 1

Mayo Clinic Staff. "Chronic Stress Puts Your Health at Risk." *Mayo Clinic*, July 8, 2021. https://www.mayoclinic.org/healthy-lifestyle/stress-management/in-depth/stress/art-20046037.

The Ripple Effect. "Daniel Goleman's Explanation of 'Amygdala Hijacks.'" December 18, 2020. Video, 3:34. https://www.youtube.com/watch?v=GHnuyJFGVng.

CHAPTER 2

Cooperrider, D.L., and Whitney, D. *A Positive Revolution in Change: Appreciative Inquiry*. Taos, NM: Corporation for Positive Change, 1999.

Lewis, Julie, and Darlene Van Tiem. "Appreciative Inquiry: A View of a Glass Half Full." *Performance Improvement*. 43,8: 19-24.

Manzoni, Jean-Francois and Jean-Louis Barsoux. "The Set-Up-To-Fail Syndrome." *Harvard Business Review*, March–April, 1998. https://hbr.org/1998/03/the-set-up-to-fail-syndrome.

Ovid, and Allen Mandelbaum. *The Metamorphoses of Ovid*. New York: Harcourt Brace, 1993.

Shaw, George Bernard. *My Fair Lady*. New York: Simon & Schuster, Enhanced Classics Edition, 2005.

Suskind, Ron. *A Hope in the Unseen: An American Odyssey from the Inner City to the Ivy League*. New York: Broadway Books, 1998.

CHAPTER 3

Beilfuss, Lisa. "Covid Drove Workers to Quit. Here's Why From the Person Who Saw It Coming." *Barron's*, December 30, 2021. Updated January 3, 2022. https://www.barrons.com/articles/covid-worker-shortage-great-resignation-professor-what-comes-next-51640853004.

Business Wire Staff. "Colonial Life Study: Stressed Workers Costing Employers Billions—Weekly." *Business Wire*, March 14, 2019. https://www.businesswire.com/news/home/20190314005804/en/Colonial-Life-study-Stressed-workers-costing-employers-billions-%E2%80%93-weekly.

Cascio, Jamais. "Facing the Age of Chaos." *Medium*, April 29, 2020. https://medium.com/@cascio/facing-the-age-of-chaos-b00687b1f51d.

Gallup. "Americans' Mental Health Ratings Sink to New Low." 2022. https://news.gallup.com/poll/327311/americans-mental-health-ratings-sink-new-low.aspx.

Gallup. "US Employee Engagement Data Hold Steady in First Half of 2021." 2022. https://www.gallup.com/workplace/352949/employee-engagement-holds-steady-first-half-2021.aspx.

Indeed. "Employee Burnout Report: COVID-19's Impact and 3 Strategies to Curb It." 2021.
https://www.indeed.com/lead/preventing-employee-burnout-report.

Insider Intelligence. "US Ecommerce Growth Jumps to More than 30%, Accelerating Online Shopping Shift by Nearly 2 Years." 2020.
https://www.emarketer.com/content/us-ecommerce-growth-jumps-more-than-30-accelerating-online-shopping-shift-by-nearly-2-years.

Jezior, Melissa and Bitina Amin. "COVID-19 and Employee Burnout: Maintaining Focus, Productivity, and Engagement." April 15, 2020. Webinar. Produced by Eagle Hill Consulting.
https://www.eaglehillconsulting.com/wp-content/uploads/EHC-COVID-19-and-Employee-Burnout-Webinar.pdf.

Kaiser Family Foundation. "Mental Health Impact of the COVID-19 Pandemic: An Update." 2021.
https://www.kff.org/coronavirus-covid-19/poll-finding/mental-health-impact-of-the-covid-19-pandemic.

Owl Labs. "State of Remote Work 2019." 2019.
https://resources.owllabs.com/state-of-remote-work/2019.

Oxford Essential Quotations. 4th Edition. s.v. "Helmuth von Moltke 1800–91 Prussian Military Commander." Accessed February 21, 2022.
https://www.oxfordreference.com/view/10.1093/acref/9780191826719.001.0001/q-oro-ed4-00007547.

Reynolds, Brie Weiler. "FlexJobs, Mental Health America Survey: Mental Health in the Workplace." *FlexJobs,* 2022.
https://www.flexjobs.com/blog/post/flexjobs-mha-mental-health-workplace-pandemic.

Schaufeli, W.B. "Burnout: A Short Socio-Cultural History." In *Burnout, Fatigue, Exhaustion,* edited by Neckel, S., Schaffner, A., Wagner, G. Palgrave, 105–127. London: Palgrave Macmillan, 2017.

Tom Scott. "Why the Dutch Headwind Cycling Championships Are Difficult and Amazing." February 10, 2020. Video, 2:43.
https://www.youtube.com/watch?v=VMinwf-kRlA.

UMass Memorial Health. "Everyone Experiences Stress. It's a Part of the Human Experience." 2022.
https://www.ummhealth.org/center-mindfulness.

World Health Organization. "Burn-Out an 'Occupational Phenomenon': International Classification of Diseases." 2022.
https://www.who.int/news/item/28-05-2019-burn-out-an-occupational-phenomenon-international-classification-of-diseases.

CHAPTER 4

Association for Psychological Science (APS). "Shared Pain Brings People Together." 2014. https://www.psychologicalscience.org/news/releases/shared-pain-brings-people-together.html.

Khazan, Olga. "The Importance of Sharing Experiences." *The Atlantic.* October 16, 2014. https://www.theatlantic.com/health/archive/2014/10/the-importance-of-sharing-experiences.

Sheldrake, Merlin. *Entangled Life: How Fungi Make Our Worlds, Change our Minds, and Shape our Futures.* New York: Random House, 2020.

Sting. "Sting Discusses My Songs—Message in A Bottle." December 5, 2019. Video, 1:27. https://www.youtube.com/watch?v=bH_CU56Yv_0.

CHAPTER 6

Brach, Tara. *Radical Acceptance: Enhancing Your Life with the Heart of a Buddha.* New York: Bantam Books, 2003.

Rinne, April. *Flux: 8 Superpowers for Thriving in Constant Change.* Oakland, CA: Berret-Koehler, 2021.

University of Texas Austin. "A Carrot, an Egg, and a Cup of Coffee." 2022. http://sites.edb.utexas.edu/resilienceeducation/inspiring-stories/a-carrot-an-egg-and-a-cup-of-coffee.

CHAPTER 7

Abrashoff, Michael. *It's Your Ship: Management Techniques from the Best Damn Ship in the Navy.* New York: Warner Books, 2002.

Ewjxn. "1985 Dry Idea Antiperspirant TV Commercial Never Let Them See You Sweat." September 11, 2017. Video, 0:29. https://youtu.be/FvDmOPmog_4.

LaBarre, Polly. "The Agenda—Grassroots Leadership" *Fast Company*, March 31, 1999. https://www.fastcompany.com/36897/agenda-grassroots-leadership.

Lichty, George. Cartoon of Airplane Pilot Addressing Passengers. *Collier's Weekly*, October 11, 1947.

CHAPTER 8

Laloux, Frederic. *Reinventing Organizations: A Guide to Creating Organizations Inspired by the Next Stage in Human Consciousness.* Brussels: Nelson Parker, 2014.

CHAPTER 9

Anthony, Scott, Alasdair Trotter and Evan Schwartz. "The Top 20 Business Transformations of the Last Decade." *Harvard Business Review*, September 24, 2019. https://hbr.org/2019/09/the-top-20-business-transformations-of-the-last-decade.

Franklin, Ralph W., editor. *The Poems of Emily Dickinson*. Cambridge, MA: Harvard University Press, 1999.

Hollywood Reporter. "Golden Globes: Read Ricky Gervais' Scathing Opening Monologue." 2020. https://www.hollywoodreporter.com/news/general-news/transcript-ricky-gervais-golden-globes-2020-opening-monologue-1266516.

Statista. "US Existing Home Sales 2005–2023." 2021. https://www.statista.com/statistics/226144/us-existing-home-sales.

Statista. "US Party and Event Planner Industry Market Size 2011–2021." 2021. https://www.statista.com/statistics/1176483/party-and-event-planner-industry-market-size-us.

The World Counts. "How Many Babies are Born a Day?" 2022. https://www.theworldcounts.com/challenges/toxic-exposures/polluted-bodies/how-many-babies-are-born-a-day.